Dear Jason,

A very happy b
brings back sor
Much love
Guy + Simon

The early years of hospital radio at The Royal Marsden

Radio Marsden

David Peschier

The early years of hospital radio at The Royal Marsden

Radio Marsden

Published by DPHP Publishing

peschier.publishing@yahoo.com

Paperback ISBN - 978-1-9196351-0-1
eBook ISBN - 978-1-9196351-1-8

Printed in the United Kingdom

Cover design and layout by www.spiffingcovers.com

For Diana, with love.

Acknowledgements

Daughter Francesca, and my friend Andrew Perkins, for their help and encouragement in choosing the book cover.

Alan Hart, for his permission to reproduce his Radio Marsden logo.

James Pringle, for his consent to include a number of his photographs.

The Advertiser, for the photographs featuring John Cleese

Gabriel, Stefan, Liz and the rest of the Spiffing Covers team for their help, advice and professional wisdom in bringing my book to publication.

Contents

Introduction

In 2019, Radio Marsden, the voluntary hospital broadcasting service of The Royal Marsden Hospital, Sutton, Surrey celebrated its 50th birthday. Having founded the service in 1969, I was delighted to be invited along to celebrate this milestone and have the opportunity to meet its current members as well as a few remaining from the time I was there. I had been involved with Radio Marsden for 22 years of my life and was immensely proud of the fact it had not only survived for half a century but flourished in a time which had seen many changes in the way hospital patients receive their entertainment. They are now able to access television, music and social media through their mobile phones, laptops and tablets, none of which existed when Radio Marsden started and were still in their infancy by the time I left. In the early seventies, a patient's main alternative to listening to the hospital's own radio service was to have a cassette player such as the Sony Walkman. A television set was usually located in each section of the ward but placed high above the entrance door – this made viewing difficult and programme choice would be decided by majority vote. A lack of alternative entertainment gave hospital radio services like Radio Marsden the chance to be of real benefit to patients and to lift their mood. It was, and remains to this day, something to take their minds off their illness, as well as the discomfort and side effects often caused by the treatment itself.

The Royal Marsden is one of the world's most influential

hospitals for the diagnosis and treatment of all forms of cancer. This was even more the case in the early seventies, when significant advances were being made in chemotherapy medicines. These were often administered alongside the more conventional use of radiotherapy and surgery. Along with the Institute of Cancer Research, located on the same Sutton site, the two organisations combine to form a unique partnership, rated to this day as one of the top cancer centres globally.

Every patient I met during my many years at The Royal Marsden – whether they be young or old – filled me with respect. Younger patients were the bravest, just getting on with their lives when that very life itself was threatened by their illness. I dedicate this book to all the patients of The Royal Marsden Hospital and salute their bravery and stoicism. Not just in the way they fought their illnesses but also by putting up with Radio Marsden in the days before it was finally fashioned into a decent radio service. Those early listeners were often our sternest critics but whatever they said was done with a smile on their faces and they always tuned in with great enthusiasm to whatever programme or special show we were doing. During my 22 years at Radio Marsden, getting on for a hundred volunteers joined the service at various times as we expanded our broadcasting hours before we eventually linked up with The Royal Marsden in Fulham, who recruited their own programme teams. Many volunteers stayed for a good number of years before work or personal commitments led them to decide to move on. A few gained employment in professional radio or other branches of entertainment. One or two of them were still at Radio Marsden when I returned to help celebrate its landmark 50th birthday. Despite there being a large number of them, apart from photo captions, I have decided to name just two in this book. Firstly, Graham Banks, my school friend who I coerced into helping set up the station, having suddenly realised the enormity of the task I had got myself involved in. Secondly, Andrew Robertson, who played such a major part in turning a very amateur hospital radio into a pretty good one by laying the foundations that would lead to it still broadcasting 50 years later. To them and all those other Radio Marsden volunteers, my thanks again for the parts you all played and the time you devoted to presenting, assisting and maintaining the service. I apologise for not mentioning you all, but I have listed as many as I could remember at the end of this book and am sorry if any of you have been accidentally omitted. My time at the hospital was helped in no small way by the amazing cooperation received from all the hospital staff, administrators, doctors, nurses, porters and, not forgetting the Physics Department, who built our first studio equipment.

Since the 1990s, the number of voluntary hospital radio stations has been falling as it has become easier for patients to access their own choice of radio, TV, films or games through smart phones, laptops, tablets and portable DVD players, so becoming less dependent on a hospital radio service for their entertainment needs.

Hospital radio continues to have a future, as long as it is accessible and the volunteers are always in direct touch with the patients it serves. The original concept of a hospital radio only broadcasting live from a studio is slowly being replaced by many – including Radio Marsden – installing computer play-out systems. These enable presenters to create programmes from their homes which are then stored and broadcast at a later date. This gives rise to many stations now being able to broadcast 24 hours a day, 7 days a week, theoretically without any volunteers having to be there. Thankfully, that is not the case and some programmes continue to be broadcast live from the studio at various times during the day and in the evenings. Whether this sophisticated use of technology is progress depends on which school of hospital radio you belong to. Old school will look on it as a backward step but those new to hospital radio will see it as its future. The same applies to broadcasting on the internet, which many stations now do. Is that a step too far from its remit or one to be welcomed as it brings it to a wider audience? After all, most local radio stations now do it, so it's no surprise when a station such as BBC Radio London suddenly has a listener phoning in from as far away as Toronto or Sydney! Having started Radio Marsden from scratch over half a century ago, I know at which end of its history I am entrenched in, but I still do my best to see the positives in all the changes. Whether anyone could or would start a hospital radio in this day and age is very doubtful. According to the best estimates, over 350 hospital radio services were operating across the UK in the early eighties. By comparison, the current number registered with the Hospital Broadcasting Association is down to around 170. A lot of this reduction in numbers is attributed to hospitals themselves amalgamating or being rebuilt without planners giving thought to provide a studio for a voluntary radio service. Every hospital radio these days is faced with funding the very expensive costs associated with the high level of sophisticated technical equipment required if they intend to broadcast their programmes 24/7. Across the country, reductions and changes in the structure of a hospital's management makes it more difficult for volunteers to arrange meetings with them. The consequences of such changes often result in decisions on proposed ideas taking an age to come through, which can affect the morale of those involved. It's a long way from how it used to work when Radio Marsden was starting out. A lot of progress would be achieved through a short meeting with the hospital's administrator or the chief electrician and it is hard to imagine any hospital these days actually building the equipment for such a service, as happened in my case. The now old-fashioned concept of a hospital providing free televisions and a radio system to bring programmes to a bedside unit is no more. This has been replaced by commercial companies, the largest in UK being Hospedia, whose consoles are found in almost 140 hospitals and offer the patient TV, radio, films and games plus a telephone facility. However, many of these have to be paid for by the patient or their family. This strange state of affairs has come about in the last twenty years as a direct result of an Act of Parliament called *The Patient Power Project*. This was passed into law and transferred the cost of such a service to the users, the patients, freeing the responsibility and cost from the NHS. Much of Hospedia's entertainment system is chargeable to the patient, except for incoming phone calls which remain free, as is access to an existing hospital radio service. The ability for most hospital radio services to be heard on the internet not only brings them to a larger audience, but more importantly enables patients to access the programmes via their own smart phone, tablet or laptop computer.

Everything has changed since the day I tried, without success, to join an established hospital radio service leading to me starting one myself, and here is that story.

CHAPTER 1

From railway to radio

It would be wrong to say my parents had irreconcilable differences but from an early age I remember their constant verbal sparring. This was always due to Dad spending a lot of time away from home which, I later discovered, started before I was born when he served an extra year after the war helping repatriate soldiers back to Africa. My earliest memories were of his frequent month-long business trips abroad and numerous nights away from us while travelling around the country visiting his customers. All this left my mother spending a lot of time on her own, harbouring a growing resentment of Dad as he often returned from a trip – particularly the ones to the Far East – and immediately told her of the places he had visited and the great times he had there. I was conscious of this from an early age and by the time I reached my teenage years, the day he returned from overseas would soon trigger another almighty row. Their worsening relationship involved frequent shouting matches which made me really concerned that one of them might injure, or god forbid, murder the other. I know such concerns must sound a strange route to the start of a hospital radio but that's how it was for me.

When I was 14, we were, once again, moving to a new

house. This was something we did every few years, usually thanks to our improving finances but sometimes due to Mum falling-out with the neighbours as by now she was clearly suffering from depression. I was given the news that my much-cherished model railway had to go as the new house had fewer bedrooms so it could no longer have a room of its own. This was despite there still being a spare bedroom put aside to accommodate overnight visitors who were non-existent. I had always loved my railway, having received my first train set as a Christmas present when I was six. Dad had been busy for a couple of weeks, constructing what he said was going to be a door made from hardboard and wooden batons. He ignored my questions as to where this would go in our house which was already full of doors, until all became clear on Christmas Day. As well as giving me a train set, Dad also revealed his newly built 'door', miraculously transformed into a board on which was my first permanent layout of an oval of track and a couple of sidings. Each year from then on, the boards would become larger, more track would be added, with additional trains, stations and buildings given to me for birthday and Christmas presents. After ten years it had grown to a size where it occupied its own room. Relatives would arrive for a visit and the men would immediately ask 'can we see the train room?'. To say it dominated my life would be an understatement, so it was a bitter disappointment to be told it was time for it to go, especially as it had been my way of blanking-out the rows my parents continued to regularly have by allowing me to immerse myself in a train day.

By way of compensating me for the train set being sold off, Dad said I could choose something new and that's how I came to own a Grundig TK14 reel-to-reel tape recorder, complete with its flickering green magic eye which, at the time, I thought was the height of technology. After mastering how it worked, I was soon amusing myself by hiding it in the lounge whenever my parents had visitors and secretly recording them as they sat around and exchanged their boring pleasantries. It wasn't long before this got me into hot water when Aunt Flo arrived on one of her state visits. She was posh, with all the airs and graces of someone from the landed gentry, except she was not, having landed from Newton Abbot where the greatest excitement had been her daily trip to the paddock to pick out the weeds. On hearing me replay the recording of her conversation with my parents, Aunt Flo shrieked, 'That is not me boy, I do not sound anything like that!' What clearly annoyed her was, for the first time in her life, she had heard her own dropped aitches and guttural voice. Such were her protests, I was duly banished from the room, along with my offending tape recorder.

Over the following few months my parents' arguments started to subside and I no longer felt the need to be on constant alert in case called upon to provide a manslaughter trial with my recorded evidence. My Grundig was put to work recording as many radio comedy shows as I could find, along with music, usually from my favourite, Alan 'Fluff' Freeman's *Pick of the Pops*, then broadcast on the BBC's Light Programme. I added a record deck and a basic four channel mixer enabling Radio David to begin broadcasting. When I say 'broadcasting' it actually went down a line into the kitchen where Mum, my audience of one, had no other option than to listen as I had wired it into the speaker in her radio. She remained surprisingly tolerant when I forced her to give up her normal listening station in favour of my efforts. This would be followed by an interrogation about the previous hour's programme which consisted of me spouting rubbish before attempting to introduce records before the singing started. My limited stock of singles meant Mum soon grew tired of hearing me talking over the introductions to such hits such as 'Summer Holiday' or 'Glad All Over' before crashing over the first line of the vocals.

One day Dad came home with a newly purchased Kodak Super8 cine camera and soon became obsessed with filming everything – holidays, visitors to our house and even taking it away with him on his frequent business trips to Hong Kong. There he would film the harbour as he crossed it on the ferry, people he met and even a Chinese wedding he was invited to. He soon amassed a vast number of small 50-foot reels of 8mm film. It was not long before I was roped-in to edit and splice them together on a larger reel which would then run for around 30 minutes. In his earlier life, Dad had been a cinema manager and it still showed. Relatives and friends would visit to watch his films and on taking their seats in our lounge, would even receive a programme. He would insist Mum served them interval snacks and I often wondered if he would ever go one step too far by encouraging her to wear an usherette's uniform, handing her a torch and draping a tray of ice creams around her neck. Fortunately, he stopped short of this, possibly fearing another outbreak of rows between them.

A few months later, Dad bought a state-of-the art Eumig sound projector and sent away his films for a magnetic strip to be added. Again, I was enrolled as his assistant. This time I was more enthusiastic, given my own hobby of sound recording. Dad was an exceptional public speaker but detested scripts. He had become adept at giving off-the-cuff commentaries when showing his films, but it was a different matter when it came to actually recording the soundtracks, as he still refused to write his commentary before delivering it. I had to bite my tongue as take followed take. During one session, recording had stretched into the early hours of the morning, as relatives were coming later in the day for the premiere of his latest film and it had to be completed. At around the tenth attempt, with the screen showing a familiar Hong Kong scene into its closing frames, the soundtrack recording was, at last, going well, until suddenly he said, 'Thousands of people make their daily journey to work across the harbour aboard the famous Star Ferry and here is one, arriving on the Hong Kong side. Down goes the... What do you call that?' More than fifty years later, I can never near the word 'gangway' without thinking of that aborted recording. If only he had used a script, we could have had it done and dusted in no time, instead of needing to start all over again, as Dad was a perfectionist.

I continued to amuse, or more accurately irritate, Mum with my daily one-hour programme until she finally threatened to stop my pocket money if I didn't switch-off Radio David and reinstate her favourite BBC Light Programme. The wire to her radio was disconnected and so I lost my licence to broadcast to the kitchen. For the next couple of years, my time was occupied with school exams followed by going out to work. However, the onset of the BBC's Radio 1 in 1967, featuring many of the previously outlawed pirate radio DJs, made me even more interested in recording my own programmes, as well as learning how to cut and splice segments together.

I first heard of hospital radio around 1968 and thought that might be something worth getting involved in. I drew a circle on a map to show the hospitals in a five-mile radius of my home in Croydon. I sent letters out to the main ones – Mayday, St Helier, Queen Mary's Hospital for Children and The Royal Marsden in Sutton. Their replies were all negative as none had a hospital radio at that time. The only positive response was from The Royal Marsden Hospital who invited me to visit them as they thought there could be some benefits in having something like that. I had not been expecting a reply from them and really knew nothing about such a specialist hospital, so I urgently needed to do some research and quickly discovered there were actually two Royal Marsden hospitals. The original, in London's Fulham Road, was the first hospital in the world dedicated to the study and treatment of cancer. Founded as the Free Cancer Hospital in 1851 by Dr William Marsden, it was granted its Royal Charter in 1910 but not renamed The Royal Marsden until 1954. In 1963, a second Royal Marsden in Sutton was opened by Her Majesty Queen Elizabeth II in response to the need for the hospital to expand in order to treat more patients and train more doctors.

The Royal Marsden was clearly no ordinary hospital, so I was somewhat apprehensive when I went along in early 1969 to the first meeting in response to my letter. The person conducting it was Margaret Rix, the hospital's occupational therapist. We got on well right from the start and she explained how the various treatments for cancer were often more uncomfortable for the patient than the cancer itself. Patients usually received both radiotherapy and chemotherapy, a new pioneering treatment, very much in its infancy back then. The effects of both these treatments could be severe, often causing sickness, loss of hair and a feeling of constant tiredness. These debilitating impacts on a patient's general health, particularly from the chemotherapy, were generally more severe back then compared with nowadays as the knowledge about the dosages of chemotherapy needed to treat the spread of a cancer were still in their infancy. Fifty years on, these have been refined to the point where most patients feel less effect on their general health while undergoing the treatment which they usually receive as an outpatient through a course of tablets. Patients would be admitted to Pinkham Ward and stay for at least a week, receiving their daily chemotherapy injections so they could be carefully monitored and given time to recover from the side effects. All this shocked me as I had imagined that joining a hospital radio would be all about playing happy songs to new mums or to patients recovering from various non-life-threatening operations. This cancer stuff sounded way too serious. Did they really think a hospital radio could help? Just to complicate matters, Margaret told me The Royal Marsden London's own Occupational Therapy Department had been presenting a live record programme for the previous 18 months and found it successful enough to broadcast over one of the radio channels. I needed to go and see what that was all about and soon I was entering the imposing building housing the original Royal Marsden Hospital in London's Fulham Road. Their Department's staff had indeed been organising a weekly music programme in a lounge, playing tracks from their library of classical records. These were interspersed with dedications to patients. However, this was just one aspect of their therapy work rather than being a fully functioning hospital radio. They agreed that if something similar was started at Sutton, I could borrow records from their collection which they would send down on the hospital transport. That would prove very useful, as my own record collection was devoid of any classical music.

Back in Sutton, I discussed with Margaret how best we could start broadcasting, but was quickly told that was way in the future. The hospital management needed to be sure some form of music therapy would benefit patients before they could agree to them having a hospital broadcasting service similar to those operating elsewhere in the country. This was how, the yet to be named, Radio Marsden, took its first tentative steps. It was certainly not by immediately having its own radio studio broadcasting to patients' bedsides. Instead, I agreed to present a live one-hour record request programme on Tuesday evenings, with the patients coming along to hear it in a large day room on Kennaway Ward.

The idea of presenting a programme on my own in front of an audience was not what I had intended when I first wrote those letters asking to join a hospital radio, and I rather lost my nerve at the sheer idea of it. To overcome this I needed support, so I called my friend Graham Banks who I had known since junior school and, after a good few number of drinks, he agreed to join me. We discussed how best to present the programme and what equipment we would need. My old Grundig was not up to the task so I bought a Sony TC200 reel-to-reel machine, a clever piece of kit as it had detachable speakers which formed the lid and stereo channels which could take speech or music. I worked out that the best way to present the programme would be to have a microphone plugged into the left channel which I would use to make the introductions and the music could be fed through the right one. Each request would need to be recorded in advance on its own tape cassette which Graham would play in on cue from another machine. We calculated that this set-up, although very simple, would work fine, given the size of the day room, as the Sony amplifiers had sufficient power for us to be clearly heard by the 20 to 30 patients we hoped would attend. Our audience of patients could either walk in to join us, travel by wheelchair or, as happened from time to time, even arrive in their hospital beds as the day room was large enough to accommodate at least a couple of them. We were pleased to welcome everyone, no matter what their mode of hospital transport.

Record requests were collected in advance by members of the League of Friends visiting the patients on the wards. These volunteers gave us a lot of support from day one and continued to do so throughout my time at Radio Marsden. Once I had them, I would send a list of any requests for classical music to Fulham Road and their Occupational Therapy Department would send down the records to Sutton on the hospital transport. They would arrive in a big white box previously used for X-ray film and this made us feel very 'medical' as we walked through the hospital carrying it. Any requests from the current hit parade would be 'half-inched' from my weekly recording of the BBC's *Pick of the Pops*. I also bought an Elizabethan (brand not age) cassette player and would spend a lot of the weekend recording the 15 to 20 different music requests onto individual cassettes. This crazy method of presenting the programme actually worked well and Graham soon became adept at giving each cassette a quick forward wind with a pencil to ensure the music started on cue just as he pressed the play button.

On reflection, it sounds a strange way to start a hospital radio, but I could understand the caution shown by both the hospital administrator and the Occupational Therapy Department as we had yet to prove, not only our own long-term commitment, but also that the programme was of some benefit to the patients. Each Tuesday, Graham and I would transport the equipment to Sutton and unload it in the car park before carrying it up to the Kennaway Ward day room where we would spend around 30 minutes setting it all up and rearranging the chairs for our audience. All this would involve a rush home from work to get to the hospital as early as we could. Having got everything ready, there was usually just about time for our 'warm-up'. This comprised a cup of tea and a biscuit to revive ourselves and maybe a quick game of table tennis in the Occupational Therapy Department to sooth our nerves, before heading back up to Kennaway Ward to start the programme. By 6.45pm we would be sitting nervously behind a couple of tables surrounded by equipment and I recall saying to Graham that first evening, 'What if nobody turns up?' Happily, that didn't happen, and the programme was well received right from the start. In the proceeding months, we learnt a lot about the way the hospital worked, the strength and courage of the patients and a little about how to present a record programme. I am in no doubt that method of starting Radio Marsden laid the foundations which served it well from the outset and for the next 50 years. Those early 'live' programmes in front of the patients, with many of them chatting to us afterwards, were invaluable in getting to know how a full radio service could work in such a very specialist hospital.

After about three months, the hospital confirmed that our weekly programme was definitely improving patient morale and agreed to our real ambition of broadcasting the programme over the internal radio system so that all the patients throughout the hospital could hear it, rather than just those who were either sufficiently mobile or reliant on helpful ward staff to come to the Kennaway day room. The hospital administrator put us in touch with the Physics Department and authorised them to build some studio equipment to enable us to feed programmes into an existing radio channel using record decks, microphone and a mixer. While genuinely sad at the thought of ending our weekly live programme and the buzz we got from that immediate audience response, it had served us well as our apprenticeship and proved the benefit of music to the patients. We had stuck at it, but the equipment seemed to get heavier each week as we moved it from Croydon to Sutton and back, not helped by me living in a third-floor flat with no lift. The idea of starting to actually broadcast using equipment provided by the hospital became very exciting.

I had visited a few well-established hospital radio stations during our initial months at the Marsden. Each had many enthusiastic volunteers, but many of their presenters just seemed to be trying to sound as much like a Radio 1 DJ as they could. I was determined that would not happen at Radio Marsden. It also struck me that their smart studio set-ups, with their glass partitions and red glowing 'on air' lights were often located some way from the central core of their hospital. This could be somewhere in the grounds or in a basement well away from the hospital wards and main buildings. Such remoteness, while not affecting the standard of their radio broadcasting, was not helpful in forming the kind of relationship between presenters and patients we had already achieved by presenting our programme live in front of our audience. We had encouraging feedback from the patients we would talk to after each programme and that had initiated a much stronger bond than we could have achieved if we had started by talking to them through the radio from a remote location. We had undergone a steep learning curve from our experiences in the day room and knew how to interact with our patients. This proved a major factor in the way Radio Marsden would approach the change to broadcasting and it became our policy to stay in close touch with patients and visitors by always having our studio door open and, in time, presenting live programmes from the various wards.

We continued with our weekly day room programme as we waited for the Physics Department to complete building our studio equipment. They had asked what we needed and our shopping list to them comprised 'two turntables, an eight-channel mixer and a microphone please'. Anyone reading this who is familiar with radio broadcasting will know what Pre-Fade Listening (PFL) is and how it enables you to cue up a record or tape through your headphones off-air so it's ready to start the second you hit a switch. We had never heard of PFL, so it was not on our specification list. It was not long after the equipment was installed that we realised what a major blunder that had been. We were left without PFL, instead only having EFL (Ear-Fade Listening). That less sophisticated version required us to put the stylus on the record and bend our head down until our ear was almost touching it. We then moved the edges of the felt pad under the record back and forth until a sound was heard from the first groove. Half a turn back should see it cued-up and ready to play when you started the turntable. Not asking for PFL really was a very stupid mistake but this was pioneering radio at its most basic level and we still had it all to learn.

Radio David's very basic bedroom studio set-up.

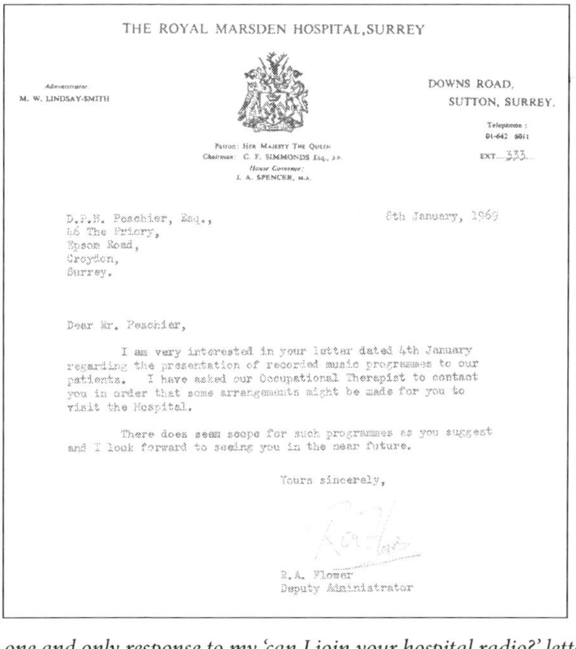

THE ROYAL MARSDEN HOSPITAL, SURREY

Administrator:
M. W. LINDSAY-SMITH

Patron: HER MAJESTY THE QUEEN
Chairman: C. F. SIMMONDS Esq., J.P.
House Governor:
J. A. SPENCER, M.A.

DOWNS ROAD,
SUTTON, SURREY.

Telephone:
01-642 6011

EXT. 333

D.P.H. Peschier, Esq.,
46 The Priory,
Epsom Road,
Croydon,
Surrey.

8th January, 1969

Dear Mr. Peschier,

I am very interested in your letter dated 4th January regarding the presentation of recorded music programmes to our patients. I have asked our Occupational Therapist to contact you in order that some arrangements might be made for you to visit the Hospital.

There does seem scope for such programmes as you suggest and I look forward to seeing you in the near future.

Yours sincerely,

R.A. Flower
Deputy Administrator

The one and only response to my 'can I join your hospital radio?' letters.

Our first live programme gets underway in the Kennaway Ward day room with Graham loading a cassette containing a pre-recorded music request.

CHAPTER 2

Let broadcasting commence

The new equipment was installed in the Staff Common Room, just off the main corridor of the hospital. This was an excellent location as every visitor and member of staff used that passageway. I thought the hospital had chosen this room to help us really be part of the hospital, but I soon realised it was just by luck as it already housed the radio transmitters in a cupboard, so was the logical choice for us to be there. We placed our equipment, which looked more like an office desk than a studio mixing console, in one corner of the room, the rest of the space being already full of lounge chairs for staff to relax in during their breaks. There was no space, or permission, to install any 'studio style' window partitioning, so it looked very unlike a proper radio studio. After a few weeks, we noticed hardly any hospital staff actually used this Common Room, preferring to relax in the restaurant during their breaks. One weekend, we decided to move a few of the chairs out and see what would happen. The following week there were no complaints from the staff or the hospital. A month or so later, we 'lost' a few more with still no ripples of discontent from anybody. Every week or so we continued to move them out one-by-one, relocating them in the hospital's various lounges until all the chairs had gone. Following on from this success, we took off the *Staff Common Room* door sign by sliding it out of its runners. We then put it back with the blank side showing and glued onto it our own *Radio Marsden Studio* sign. It stayed that way for a good few years before the carpentry department installed a completely new door for us, this one with a large window in it so passers-by could look through and see what was going on. It remains Radio Marsden's room 50 years later. I don't know what it is listed as on the hospital plans but there we remain, still on the main corridor of the hospital with easy access for patients and visitors alike.

Our newly built equipment was now installed and connected into the hospital's own system, with Radio Marsden claiming squatting rights in the Staff Common Room less than a year after taking those first tentative steps of presenting our first programme live in a day room. We were now ready to launch into proper broadcasting. The hospital's radio service, relayed to the patients' bedsides, comprised two channels, one carrying BBC Radio 4 and the other BBC Radio 2. Radio Marsden had been connected to it enabling us to go on air by throwing a switch and replacing Radio 2. This we did exactly as the pips ended ahead of the 7pm news. We even devised our own call sign, the 13-note introduction to The Seekers version of 'Island of Dreams'. We used this throughout my time at Radio Marsden and whenever I still hear it, I immediately wallow in a few seconds of nostalgia. Posters were printed and circulated round the hospital advertising our initial programmes – the *Record Request Show* on Tuesday evenings and the *Sunday Morning Pop Programme* at the weekend. Our wonderful League of Friends continued to tour the wards on our behalf, collecting patients' requests, just as they had done for our live day room programme. It is true to say Radio Marsden was beginning to take up a lot of our time and, with just the two of us running it, we were grateful for the League's help. Patients and visitors were encouraged to drop by the studio to make requests, speak on air or to just watch to see how it all worked. Actually, speaking at the same time as working the mixer controls and cueing up records, put us two very amateur broadcasters under a lot of pressure. Both Graham and I smoked in those days and, between us, could puff our way through the best part of a packet of 20 during our evening in the studio, such was the level of concentration needed. On one occasion a disaster happened – we ran out of cigarettes halfway through a programme! When it came to announcing the next record request, we mentioned the cigarette crisis and, much to our surprise, a patient quickly responded to our SOS and in minutes appeared at the studio door to offer us some of theirs. Back then, the link between smoking and lung cancer was not taken as seriously as nowadays and many members of the hospital staff smoked along with the patients. In hindsight, the very idea of putting out such an appeal for cigarettes is beyond belief, but this was a very different era.

Patient feedback was vital. To be honest, we were really awful in those early months with neither of us having any proper radio training or even DJ-ing experience, so we made plenty of mistakes. The credit for the little improvement we did make, was down to three patients in a room on Kennaway Ward. These ladies were our greatest, and probably only, fans. We would drop by the ward to visit them after each programme to be told in no uncertain terms what was good and what was bad. H, a teacher at a local village school, was a rock to the younger two, S and V. All three continued to write to us after they were discharged, and we went to see H and her husband in their idyllic cottage on the green in a rural village in Kent. Sadly, of the three, it was H who returned to the hospital a number of times and finally they were unable to save her. I still have the letter her husband wrote to us shortly after she had died and, nearly fifty years on, I still can't read it without getting a lump in my throat. H was a brave and unselfish lady who had continually kept up the morale of the two younger patients in the room. Not old herself, she had already given so much to the world. We were proud to have known her and she will never be forgotten.

During that first year, Radio Marsden continued to fulfil an important role as a diversional therapy for patients, which we and the hospital saw as its sole aim. We managed this thanks to our easily accessible ground-floor studio where we could welcome patients and visitors alike, by doing our best entertaining and by involving those on the wards during the actual broadcasts. The hospital provided us with their daily list of patients coming into the hospital, so we were able to give a name check and a warm welcome to each new arrival. A competition was introduced on the Tuesday request show, with one of us going around the wards handing out the entry forms and returning to collect them after the questions had been broadcast. This would have been impossible in a general hospital which can have 600 beds or more. The Sutton Royal Marsden then had around 140 beds, so it was just feasible to make a speedy trip round all the wards, which left you rather out of breath on your return to the studio. The winners of the quiz received only minor prizes, donated by local firms, but it gave the patients something else to take their minds off their treatments by taking part, which was a lot more valuable than the prizes on offer. We also introduced a Staff Award and would go onto a different ward each week with a portable tape recorder, looking for a patient to record a message nominating a member of staff who had been particularly kind or helpful to them. They could suggest anyone from a cleaner to a consultant and during the many years this feature was running, we never failed to find a patient eager to put someone forward. Their willingness to come up with names just showed how well the staff were doing looking after them. It is important to keep remembering these were times when many of the pioneering cancer treatments we take for granted today, were very much in their infancy. Whether the winners of our Staff Award actually enjoyed their prize of a bottle of Pomagne is another matter. Its packaging may have resembled a bottle of champagne, but it was in fact nothing more than cider. We couldn't afford the real thing and missed a trick by not thinking of writing to its maker, Bulmers, requesting a free supply in return for promoting it. The best I achieved for our Pomagne was a paltry 10% discount given as a goodwill gesture by our local off-licence. In hindsight, I should have offered its owner a mention on air in return for a larger reduction. On that subject, a few years later, when I was more knowledgeable about the link between cancer and smoking, I wrote to the various tobacco companies asking if they could give us either a donation or some prizes, other than cigarettes obviously. Maybe I should have spelt it out clearer in the letters, as all but one fell on deaf ears. The only exception being Alfred Dunhill whose reply was written on an impressive gold embossed letterhead. They gave their apologies and explained how they couldn't send us any prizes, as at that time all their donations went to yachting charities!

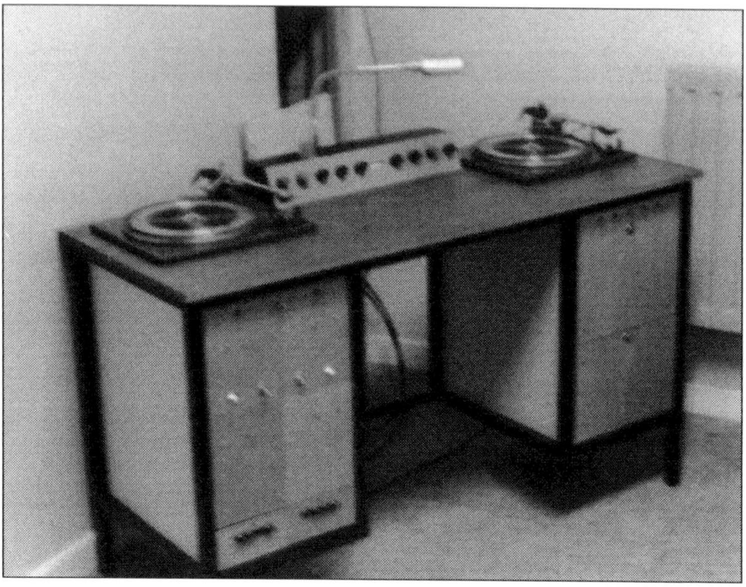

Our first studio equipment arrives, having been built by the hospital's Physics Department.

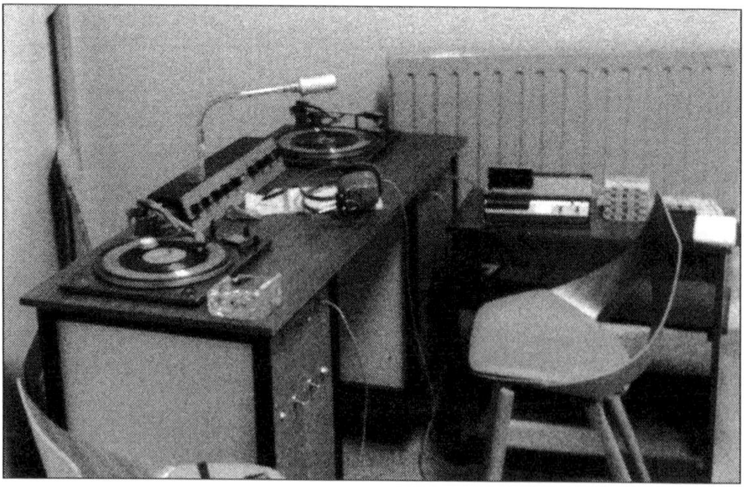

All wired-up and ready to broadcast with a few additions. A Philips cassette player and, what would now be, a very non-PC ashtray!

At last, I have the chance to say 'This is Radio Marsden broadcasting on Channel 2'.

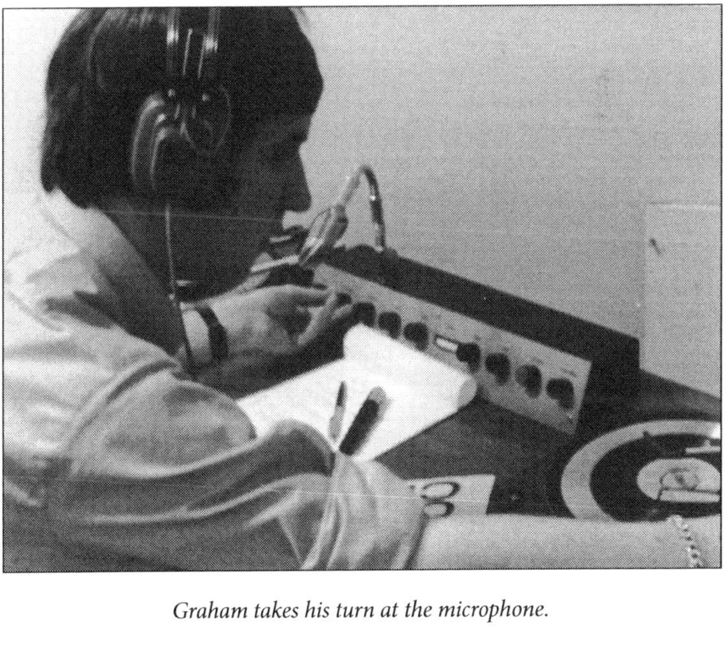

Graham takes his turn at the microphone.

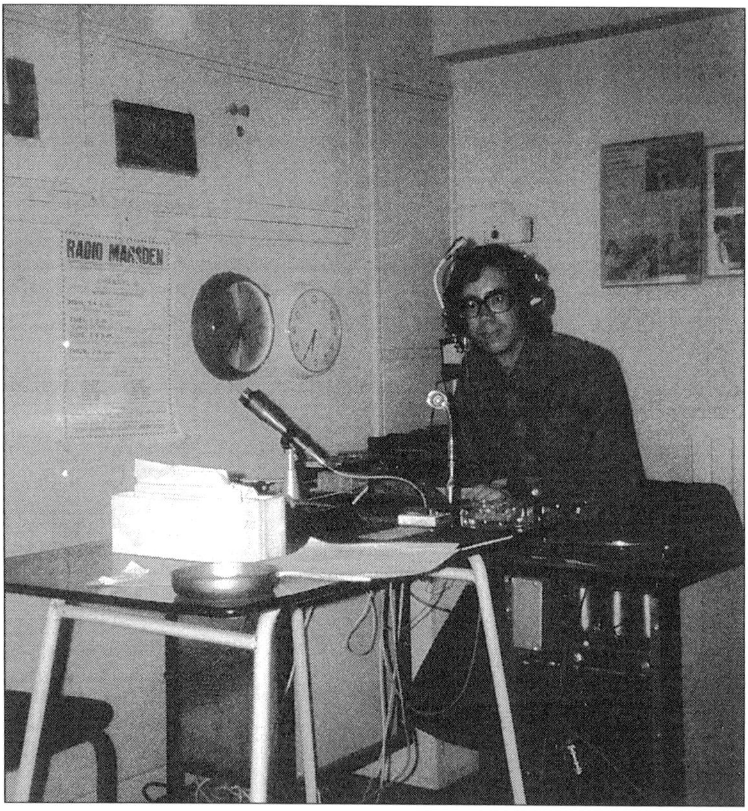

Our first sophisticated studio upgrade. Turning the desk round 90 degrees and adding a kitchen table, two clocks and an ashtray for guests!

CHAPTER 3

Our first celebrity visitors

Unlike modern times, during the 1970s you could write a letter to a celebrity and be pretty certain of receiving a reply, even though that could take a month or two. It would usually come from their agent but sometimes from the person themselves asking you to contact their PA. We decided to give it a shot without holding out much hope of success. We kept our fingers crossed they might give us an interview or, at the very best, actually agree to travel to Sutton to visit the hospital to take part in a programme. Our first positive response was from the BBC's Pat Doody, then the presenter of *Night Ride* on Radio 2, who invited us to Broadcasting House to interview him prior to presenting his show. This was our first visit to a real radio station and where better to start than at the BBC? Pat Doody was exceptionally kind and put us at ease within minutes of meeting him. He gave us a tour of the studios and, when it came to interviewing him, he clearly realised I was no David Frost. Recognising I was new to the game, he gave such long replies to each of my questions, I only got through half a dozen of the twenty or so I had written on my prompt cards before it was time to draw the interview to an end so he could go on air. That first trip to the BBC to meet a celebrity gave us a bit of confidence, but the butterflies were soon back when we read the next reply to one of the many letters we had written. That one was from Annette Andre, a beautiful blonde actress who was starring as Marty Hopkirk's widow Jeannie in the TV series *Randall and Hopkirk (Deceased)*. We agreed to alternate the interviews so this one would be Graham's. I was naturally very jealous, especially when a photo appeared in the local newspaper of him chatting to her in a very relaxed way while she had her back to me as I was stuck on the mixing desk. She was clearly out of our league, entertaining the patients with stories about her two hobbies, power-boat racing and bullfighting, and waxing lyrically about her pet Afghan hound. Annette's visit gave us our first newspaper publicity as she agreed our request to invite a reporter along from the *Sutton & Cheam Advertiser* to sit in on the programme and write an article on her visit. Following that publicity, both the *Sutton Advertiser* and its sister newspaper the *Sutton Herald* started to take a greater interest in our activities. This helped Radio Marsden gain more local recognition and some local traders responded by donating competition prizes. Another additional benefit was a solution to the chore of typing letters to personalities. This was lifted from my shoulders after a reader offered to type them for us. The newspaper publicity gained by features on our celebrity visitors also brought us an influx of new volunteers wishing to join us enabling Graham and I to start expanding our broadcasting hours.

The next visitors to Radio Marsden were our first sports stars. ITV's *Big Match* host, Brian Moore brought along John Sewell, then captain of First Division Crystal Palace FC. Not only did the pair agree to a live studio interview but also toured the wards afterwards which cheered up our male patients especially, who were pleased to see some footballer faces and bombarded them with questions.

One morning I received a telephone call from John Cleese's secretary. It was 1972 and John was already a major celebrity, having first appeared on our TV screens in *The Frost Report,* along with Ronnie Barker and Ronnie Corbett (also to take part in a Radio Marsden programme a few years later). John's stardom was further enhanced following the success of the first two series of *Monty Python's Flying Circus.* Four years later he would return to television with *Fawlty Towers,* propelling him to even greater success and world-wide recognition. His secretary explained that John was keen to help and was prepared to come down to the hospital to take part in a programme. That was great news except John didn't drive, so it was necessary for me to collect him from his house in London's St John's Wood and chauffeur him down to the hospital in Sutton. I would then drive him home again after the programme finished. John Cleese is extremely tall, 6'6", and my first concern was whether he would fit into my car, which was then a Hillman Avenger. I decided to do a test with Graham sitting in the passenger seat wearing a big hat and it all seemed OK as it didn't quite touch the roof. The next problem was how I would navigate to and from his home, this being before the invention of sat navs, leaving me dependent on road signs and, if necessary, a map. I decided a couple of reconnaissance runs in advance were vital as I was worried about the risk of being distracted. Having someone as famous as John Cleese in the passenger seat could easily result in me not concentrating on the route and heading off in the wrong direction. Having completed 'the knowledge' route between St John's Wood and Sutton two or three times the weekend before, I duly arrived outside his house at the appointed hour. When John opened his front door, my immediate thought was 6'6" was on the conservative side. He just about managed to squeeze himself into the car and his head did not touch the roof. However, it was the length of his legs that proved the problem. This was something I had not thought about when performing the 'hat test'. Sitting in my car was clearly uncomfortable for him, as even with his seat pushed as far back as possible, it still left his knees almost touching his chest. Fortunately for me, he was kind enough not to complain and we were off to Sutton. During the journey he asked what he was getting himself into that evening and I explained we would do an interview during the request show and then, if he had the time, we would like him to visit some of the wards where he could meet patients and staff and hand out a few competition prizes. He was fine with that but did say he didn't want anyone asking him to demonstrate his part as the bowler-hatted bureaucrat in Monty Python's *Ministry of Silly Walks* sketch which featured him walking around doing an extended military goose-step. Apart from *Dead Parrot,* this was probably the Python team's most memorable sketch, but John was keen not to reproduce it. I assured him that would not happen and kept my fingers crossed nobody would actually ask him. He also said he needed to be back home by 9pm which rather worried me, given the one-hour journey time and the programme starting at 7pm. I also told him a reporter from the local newspaper would be in the studio and he was happy with that when I explained that they gave us various kinds of support. On arrival at the hospital, the request show was about to begin so there was just about time to introduce him to Graham, who was working the sound desk that evening, before the programme got under way and we were on air. John proved very entertaining. You could never tell in advance how it would work out with celebrities as some are hopeless without a script, but John was happy to talk away and respond to my often-inane questions. He explained how he got into writing and performing having spent a lot of his time at university appearing alongside the likes of Jonathan Miller and Peter Cook in the famous student comedy society the Cambridge Footlights. It was there he first met David Frost, also a member of the Footlights who would go on to be the foremost TV interviewer of his generation and probably best known for TV's *That Was the Week That Was* which John had written scripts for. He entertained the Radio Marsden listeners with a tale of how he was having breakfast recently in a large hotel when a call went out – 'telephone call for Mr Cleese'. It was David calling him from Lake Tahoe, over five thousand miles away in America, just wanting to check the best way to deliver some lines John had written for him for his cabaret act. John said how he tried to keep the call short, thinking of David's phone bill but it went on and on until David said, 'Super, super, must go as back on stage in a minute.' Having returned to the hotel restaurant, the same scenario was repeated 30 minutes later with David Frost calling him again to apologise for cutting the first call short. Commenting on what had made him so successful, John explained that David Frost was a workaholic and, unlike normal people, did not need time on his own. John gave an example. 'If David Frost goes to the cinema, he does so with someone like the head of Warner Brothers.'

Having had some success with ITV's *At Last the 1948*

Show, John explained how he and his writing partner Graham Chapman were looking for another team to write alongside and that's how they found Michael Palin and Terry Jones and Eric Idle, all of whom would write and star in *Monty Python's Flying Circus*. Barry Took put the show together and John told our listeners the BBC had first given it the working title of *Barry Took's Flying Circus*. Their grey-suited executives told the writing team they had a couple of hours to come up with a final title. They all sat around making suggestions and, after many silly names had been bandied about, someone suggested 'Monty Python' for no other reason than it sounded very silly. He said they all laughed at that and it became the name of the show. With the first series so well received and a second one about to start as well as a film version, John explained how he preferred writing to performing and had some harsh words to say about his own performance in the *Dead Parrot* sketch. He blamed that on the fact the BBC only gave them two hours to rehearse when it needed at least eight.

John's own comedy inspirations came from people like Spike Milligan, as well as some of the old cinema comedians, Buster Keaton and Harold Lloyd, rather than the more obvious Charlie Chaplin. I said it had recently been reported that one of John's hobbies was 'complaining about the telephone service', he agreed it was a particular gripe of his but not a hobby. He was more content to read books or watch a game of football. I asked which team he supported, and his reply was 'whichever one is nearest to where I live at the time'. He then went on to list them as Chelsea, Torquay and West Ham as well as Bristol City having been to school at nearby Weston-Super-Mare.

Our interview hour raced along interspersed with John

reading out patients' record requests and drawing the winners of our quiz competition. Soon we were up on the wards with him meeting patients and giving out the prizes. I suddenly looked at my watch and it was already 8.45pm, mindful of his Cinderella-style wish to be home by 9pm, I gently tapped him on the shoulder to remind him of the time. 'That's OK,' he said and continued touring the wards for at least another 30 minutes. By the time I delivered him home, it was around 11pm. During the journey, he told me he would soon be making the next series of *Monty Python's Flying Circus* and to ring his secretary in a month or so if I wanted to bring a party from Radio Marsden to be in the audience to watch an episode being recorded at the BBC studios in Shepherd's Bush. Needless to say, I did exactly that and around ten of us went along for what was a thoroughly enjoyable evening. Anyone who knew the Television Centre (now sadly expensive apartments) will recall it was a circular building. We left the studio after the show recording and walked around the corridor towards the exit. A door ahead of us opened and out came John with a couple of colleagues and headed towards us. My immediate thought was, 'Oh my god, do I say anything to him?' but before I could decide, John looked at me and said, 'Hello David, did you and everyone from the hospital enjoy the recording?' I nearly fell through the floor at the thought such a star actually recognised me, and I fell further when he said, 'Do you all have time for a drink?' He promptly shepherded us upstairs to the BBC Club and asked what we would all like, before going to the bar to order. He then had a chat with everyone before we left for home with us all walking out of the BBC feeling on cloud nine. John went on to perform in a number of films in addition to writing and starring in *Fawlty Towers* along with his wife, later to become his ex-wife, Connie Booth. I will never forget what a fantastic person he was to meet and the boost to our morale he gave to everyone from being in his company, either during his visit to the hospital or when we went to see the recording.

The visit from John Cleese was closely followed by Roy Hudd, a famous TV and radio star and an expert on the music hall days. His first response to one of our letters had been to invite myself and Graham to London's Palace Theatre where he was appearing in a show starring the singer and entertainer Danny La Rue. Roy was a delight to talk to and I have included that meeting with him in my favourite interviews chapter. I had asked him afterwards if there was any chance of him coming to Sutton to take part in a programme and visit some patients. He readily agreed and said it would be easy for him to do that once the show had finished its run. He was born and bred a Croydon boy, but at that time lived in Streatham which was still fairly close to Sutton. He kept to his word and a few months later his manager drove him over to visit us. Roy never stopped smiling and entertaining us throughout the programme and it was the same when he went up to the wards. He just had a natural ability to make friends with everyone he met, a true entertainer if there ever was, having found huge success on radio, TV and the stage. He worked well into his eighties, both on stage in pantomimes, straight acting and popping up on our TV screens from time to time playing undertaker Archie Shuttleworth in *Coronation Street*.

In addition to being one of Britain's foremost stage and radio entertainers, he had always been a strong supporter of hospital radio, holding honorary titles at both Bristol and

Sandwell Hospital Radio, bestowed on him in recognition of his active support over many years. Following on from John Cleese, Roy also agreed to become a patron of Radio Marsden and we soon had sufficient celebrity names to include an impressive list on our letterhead. This we hoped would entice others to agree to be interviewed or even make a visit to us at the hospital, having seen the list of those whose footsteps they would be following!

Many of the best Radio Marsden interviews were not with celebrities, but with no lesser 'stars', our patients. This was particularly so of the children. Prior to having their own Princess Chula Ward, we had a few children being treated in a section on the adults' Miles Ward. During a visit to collect record requests, I was pleased I had our portable recorder with me as one young girl was very keen to be interviewed. She wanted to complain bitterly that she never had spaghetti like she used to have at home. Shortly after we broadcast her interview, someone tipped-off the chef and he arranged for her to be served her favourite pasta.

One day I had a call from the administrator's assistant, asking me to drop by the office to see him when I was next in the hospital. I was worried Radio Marsden may have done something wrong. When I entered his office, my eyes immediately settled on an enormous scale model of the hospital sitting under its clear plastic cover. Speaking across his huge desk, the administrator explained that a VIP patient had been admitted but it was imperative Radio Marsden did not approach him or make any reference to his presence in the hospital during our broadcasts. I asked him, who was this person? He lent across to ensure he could not be overheard and, in a very solemn voice, whispered 'Nixon'. I was shocked and could hardly manage to stutter out a reply. 'Oh my god, Richard Nixon the president of the United States?' 'No no,' he replied, 'David Nixon, the magician and TV personality.' I was less impressed on hearing that, despite the fact it was true he was the most famous magician in the UK and a well-known face on TV. Composing myself, I promised Radio Marsden would not approach him, which was a pity, but then again, he was best known for his sleight of hand card tricks and they would have been difficult to replicate on the radio.

During the following 20 years there were interviews with some really big stars, sometimes in interesting locations, which on one occasion proved positively dangerous. We enjoyed using our spare time going around talking to the various celebrities who responded. Without exception, all of the personalities we met to interview were helpful and understanding when faced with us inexperienced and amateur hospital radio volunteers. We had an almost 100% reply rate, with one exception, Harry Secombe who lived in nearby Cheam. I wrote to him numerous times, twice hand-delivering my letter. On the second occasion, a nurse from the children's Princess Chula Ward agreed to accompany me to add more credibility. We walked up the drive to his house to hand in our letter, passing Harry's Rolls Royce displaying its HS 92 number plate. I hoped, as I had the first time, maybe the great man himself would open the door but again it wasn't to be. We knocked, hopefully, and someone accepted the letter. A few weeks later, I received a reply saying Mr Secombe was about to travel to Australia for a tour and it would not be possible to do either an interview or arrange a studio visit. I kept sending in letters from time to time but nothing ever came of them. I gave up after a couple of years and my family became tired of me muttering 'never gave me an interview', whenever he appeared on the television or radio. Doing the request show, I would cringe each time I was forced to play 'If I Ruled the World', sadly one of our most requested records. Harry Secombe was our local, world-famous, celebrity, living just a couple of miles away from the hospital. I never understood why he couldn't give Radio Marsden even ten minutes of his time for an interview. It was disappointing from such a much-respected star.

Another celebrity never to be heard on Radio Marsden was Jimmy Savile and clearly that was for the good. I didn't even write to Savile as always felt there was something sinister about him, despite his tremendous TV success and general popularity. Little did I know at the time how right my inclinations were to prove over forty years later. While researching this book, I found a report of an enquiry held by The Royal Marsden after rumours that Savile had visited the hospital. They found no evidence that he had, so it was a good job I followed my original thoughts.

Graham gets all the luck – interviewing the beautiful actress Annette Andrea, leaving me to look on enviously.

Two celebrities for the price of one. We expected Brian Moore, ITV's football commentator and host of The Big Match, *but he also brought along John Sewell, captain of Division 1 team, Crystal Palace.*

The fabulous actor and comedian John Cleese visiting Radio Marsden and making us all laugh.

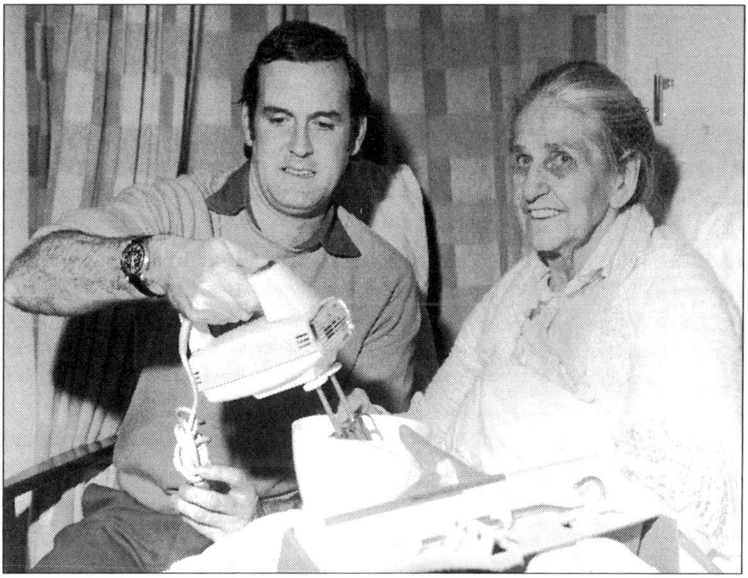

John turns a patient's prize into a practical cookery demonstration.

CHAPTER 4

We can't do all this on our own

By 1971 we were in our second year of broadcasting and enjoying every minute of it. Despite not having audiences the size of a general hospital, we, like all its staff, were proud of The Royal Marsden and the bravery and courage of its 150 patients. Our open-door policy was appreciated by everyone in the hospital and, in turn, we had been granted the right to access nearly all the hospital areas with only a few places out of bounds, such as medical records and the high voltage radiation treatment rooms. For our own protection, there was a short time when Radio Marsden volunteers had to wear radiation monitoring badges which were checked and exchanged for new ones every month. Fortunately, we never suffered any high levels of contamination, but it was a sign of how important they considered such things. Radio Marsden was well supported by all the staff in the hospital and from time to time, after our evening's programme, the administrator would drop by our studio with an invitation to join him in his office for a late-night whisky. At other times, on the way out of the hospital, we would stop for a long chat about football or politics with a night porter. Everyone working in the hospital had the same feeling there was something very special and pioneering going on at that time. There was always media coverage about The Royal Marsden with constant news reports of breakthroughs in various cancer treatments, particularly for leukaemia. In the early days of Radio Marsden, there was a four-bed unit on Miles Ward where patients, often children, would be treated inside a large transparent 'bubble' draped over their bed. This was an early form of barrier nursing. A patient could be treated while in clinical isolation, which was necessary to protect them as their immune system was compromised by the effects of the medications, reducing their body's ability to fight infections. Having the patient separated from other people reduced this risk to a minimum.

Thanks to some serious fundraising by his executors, a special ward was constructed at Sutton in memory of comedian Bud Flanagan who lost a son to leukaemia. We were still allowed to visit the patients in that ward but had to talk to them through the glass, as if they themselves were in a studio of their own. Staff and visitors wore protective clothing when having any contact with them. Many of those patients were children or young people suffering from forms of leukaemia which had previously been terminal. Thanks to these new pioneering treatments, breakthroughs were at last being made and starting to prove successful. Nowadays 90 per cent or more cases of childhood leukaemia are fully survivable thanks to the use of chemotherapy, stem cell transplants and other treatments.

The Royal Marsden in Sutton was opened by Her Majesty Queen Elizabeth II on 20th May 1963, just six years before I wrote my original letter. By 1971 it was being rapidly expanded and similarly, by then, Radio Marsden had reached the point where it could no longer continue as a two-man hospital radio service as the amount of time we were spending on it was beginning to have a detrimental effect on our day jobs. Graham and I agreed the time had come to find some new volunteers to spread the work, at the same time giving us the opportunity to expand our broadcasting hours.

We were fortunate that among the first batch of new recruits to come through our studio door was Andrew Robertson. Andrew lived locally in Cheam and was a trainee cameraman at the BBC. Similar to me, he was an only child and whereas my hobby had always been radio, his was film-making. However, he also possessed technical knowledge of sound through his BBC training and had fantastic enthusiasm. Andrew took one look at our broadcasting equipment and winced. I remember saying to him, 'Yes, OK but you work at the BBC so don't keep shaking your head over the lack of Pre-Fade Listening, that's what our ears are for!' The recruitment went well and soon we were able to expand our programmes to four evenings a week as well as add a Sunday morning show. Our immediate priority was to improve our studio equipment to correct its many shortcomings due to our lack of knowledge when it was first built. With Andrew 'knowing about these things', we were soon on a mission to raise some money and, in a few months, had sufficient to say a nostalgic farewell to the hospital-built unit that had launched Radio Marsden and replace it with a proper Alice sound mixing desk. Neither Graham nor I were technically minded, as had been clearly demonstrated in the way we had cobbled together our original equipment for the live Kennaway Ward day room programme, so it was sensible to leave it to Andrew and a few of his like-minded friends to refit the studio. Two Technics record decks and a couple of their cassette players were added to the new mixer along with some professional microphones and a top of the range Revox reel-to-reel tape recorder. They even installed a small television which had the Ceefax news information service which we soon found to be particularly useful. Our policy was not to feature any news bulletins in our programmes even though we could have done that easily by reading off the Ceefax headlines from the TV screen, because as most news was bad news, we felt reading it out as part of our programme schedule would be of no benefit to our patients' recovery or their mood. However, there were two occasions in 1981 when having the Ceefax news service came into its own. The first was in March of that year, following the shooting of President Reagan. That event occurred during the afternoon in Washington DC, making it early evening with us. The Ceefax news page flashed up the story which we followed until it became clear the president had survived the attempted assassination, despite being shot six times. We then made that announcement on air to allay the fears of any patients who may have already heard news of the shooting, maybe from a visitor or the TV, and were probably thinking the president was dead. We made the same decision a few months later when news broke of the attempted assassination of Pope John Paul II in St Peter's Square. Once again, when it was clear he had survived the attempt on his life, we announced that on air to put patients' minds at rest.

The very best piece of new studio equipment proved to be something fairly small. An atomic clock was installed, replacing our two original cheap kitchen versions which had been far from reliable. This atomic clock was updated by radio signals and its accuracy was amazing, said to only vary by one second in 100 million years! No longer did we have any excuses for frequently crashing over the 10pm pips at the end of our evening's programme when trying to seamlessly hand the Radio Marsden audience back to BBC Radio 2. Previously, our timing would be done by phoning the speaking clock shortly before starting our programme and matching one of our old clocks to its time as close as we could. However, three hours later it would have lost at least 15 seconds, making it impossible to achieve a smooth handover by making the switch over just ahead of the first pip. This timing issue had been a problem since our very first broadcast and I remember writing to Jack de Manio, then a BBC radio presenter on Radio 4's *Today*, their early morning current affairs programme. Jack was famous for often getting the time wrong which he usually blamed on the clock in the studio. In my letter I asked him if Radio Marsden could have it and he replied saying it would not be of help to us as the dial was too difficult to read which caused his own frequent mistakes. Timekeeping is so important to good radio that I still find myself regularly shouting at Radio 4's *Today* programme whenever a presenter crashes the 9 am pips. Sadly, this is still a regular occurrence as they scramble to exit the programme after the final interview has overrun.

Along with the new equipment came more volunteers, enabling us to introduce additional programmes. By now we were broadcasting on air 7–10pm Monday to Thursday and at the weekend with our *Sunday Morning Pop Show*. Sadly, that one didn't last long as there were so few listeners. Unlike general hospitals, most of our patients who were well enough to travel, were allowed home for the weekend to give them a change of scene and an opportunity to catch up with their families. They would return on Sunday evening, ready to continue their treatment the following day. Once we realised this, we discontinued the Sunday programme and put all our efforts into Monday to Thursday evenings. With it proving so popular on Tuesdays, we added a second request programme on Thursdays. Despite there being thousands of record requests throughout my time at Radio Marsden, year after year, those most requested remained the same.

Radio Marsden's most requested records 1969–1991

'My Way' – Frank Sinatra

'Green, Green Grass of Home' – Tom Jones

'What a Wonderful World' – Louis Armstrong

'I Love you Because' – Jim Reeves

'Stranger on the Shore' – Acker Bilk

'Bridge over Troubled Waters' – Simon & Garfunkel

'If I Ruled the World' – Harry Secombe

Initially, we were sensitive to playing records such as Tom Jones's 'Green, Green Grass of Home' as it was about a condemned prisoner in his final hours. Even more worrying for us was Simon & Garfunkel's popular theme to *The Graduate*, 'The Sound of Silence', as it had the line 'silence like a cancer grows' which we thought might depress our patients. Rules as to what we should and shouldn't play were discussed at length and we soon decided we had initially been over-sensitive in not wanting to play these tracks and definitely should do so when they were requested. Our only rule from then on was to exclude anything containing offensive language. The week started with *Monday-Go-Round*, a very busy programme and I still have an old copy of its running order which lists 48 items in the one-hour show! We would welcome all the new patients from a list provided by the administrator's office. As well as music, it featured interviews recorded with patients and hospital staff, comedy tracks, celebrity birthdays, a list of the bestselling books, as well as a piece of music requested by a member of the hospital staff. We also played trailers promoting the rest of the week's programmes which each team would prepare themselves.

Andrew Robertson became not only our first technical office but also Radio Marsden's programme controller. He was responsible for making a number of our early programme jingles and was a hard taskmaster. I remember one recording session at his parents' home where he had fashioned a makeshift home studio in his bedroom. This was where we made one of our first trailers designed to encourage patients to ask their family and friends to bring in any of their unwanted records and donate them to Radio Marsden. Andrew decided that 'Help' by The Beatles would be well suited to this and together we wrote a short script (necessary so as not to recall my nightmare of recording that Hong Kong film with my father all those years earlier). Our 'Help trailer' went something like this:

(me) 'Radio Marsden needs your?'
(Beatles) 'Help!'
(me) 'Radio Marsden needs your, what do you call it?'
(Beatles) 'Help!'
(me) 'Radio Marsden needs your, oh you must know?'
(Beatles) 'Herr-herr-help!'

(me) 'Yes, Radio Marsden is looking for any records you or your friends may like to donate' … and on and on it went.

Andrew insisted it had to be exactly right and I lost count of the number of takes it took until he was finally happy with the end result.

Monday-Go-Round would be followed by *Showcase*, an hour featuring drama and comedy. Wednesday had its *Take It Easy* programme which included a weekly competition requiring its presenters to rush around all the wards, handing out entry forms and returning to collect them after the questions had been aired. Lucky winners would receive a strange array of prizes, often of little or no use to them stuck in a hospital bed. It was more the taking part than the winning and such was its popularity, it eventually had its very own programme *Wednesday Winners*. Clearly ahead of our time, one programme had a weekly opinion poll feature involving more frantic dashes around the wards with voting slips. Reporters from the *Sutton Advertiser* contributed features on local news and often came into the studio and took part in programmes. To fill the last hour of each evening we introduced our *Nightcap* programme. A medley of relaxing music and poetry designed to help our patients drift off to sleep.

Andrew was a perfectionist and both Radio Marsden and our listeners benefited by him vastly improving our standard of broadcasting, which, after our very shaky start, was not difficult to achieve! His wish was to have everything as close to perfection as possible and to try new ideas such as broadcasting some programmes live from the wards. These needed a lot of extra set-up time but thanks to his BBC shift hours, Andrew was often able to be at the hospital in the afternoon to make a start installing the equipment on an upstairs ward. I would usually arrive around 5, just in time for the cables to be installed. These would need to be run from the ward hosting the programme, fed out of the nearest corridor window and dropped down onto the flat roof on the ground floor where they would finally be threaded through our studio's small fanlight window and connected to our equipment. To achieve this involved me, being taller than Andrew, climbing out of a window in the corridor and dropping down onto the flat roof to gather up the cables, pulling them across it before feeding them in through our studio window. I often wondered what patients and visitors must have thought was going on, as I regularly witnessed a look of horror on their faces as they watched me appearing to 'end it all' by climbing out of an upstairs window, as they didn't know there was a flat roof a couple of feet below. Some must have thought, 'don't panic, the treatment won't be that bad'. I was amazed that in all the times I exited the window, nobody ever approached me with a restraining hand.

The patients could listen to their bedside radio through what they called a pillow phone. This was not actually a pillow, but a small speaker built into a piece of moulded plastic which had to be held up to the ear as you would a telephone receiver. The design of this made it very uncomfortable for the patient to use compared with putting on traditional headphones. Their low volume also made them difficult to hear if the patient was trying to listen while lying down with their head on a pillow. They were uncomfortable to use if sitting up in bed as they would have to hold it to their ear with one hand, as you would do a telephone. The pillow phone was fed by a single air tube from the bedside control panel rather than being wired in. These tubes were similar to those used at the time for aircraft entertainment systems. I discovered this myself on a business flight and took more than a normal interest in how they worked. The in-flight entertainment system was fed into the headphones by connecting their two tubes into a socket in the armrest. Each tube was close to the diameter of the single one on the hospital pillow phones. These aircraft versions were far more comfortable to wear when sitting up. I demonstrated this to the hospital management having 'borrowed' a pair when I left the plane and they agreed we could replace all the pillow phones with these stethoscope-type headphones. I set about tracking down a supplier near Heathrow Airport and made a deal to buy 200 sets from them which, after a little bit of adaption, could be made to fit the single tube connection at the bedside tables. We installed them by every bed and the patients really appreciated the fact they could now listen to radio programmes without having to constantly hold a pillow phone to their ear.

Another problem we solved was how to have some kind of reminder so the patients would tune-in at 7pm to listen to us. The voluntary record request collectors went round the wards during the day telling the patients what time in the evening our programme would start and how to switch their bedside radio to Channel 2. We still needed something else to prompt them to listen to us as we had competition from the communal televisions located high up on a shelf above the entrance to each side ward. The position of the screen often made it difficult for people to see it, as this was before the arrival of the large LED televisions we watch nowadays. Portable computers and hand-held tablets were non-existent, and the height of sophistication was to have a Sony Walkman and a stock of cassettes. The lack of modern-day entertainment equipment was good for Radio Marsden, but how to give the patients a reminder to tune-in to us? One day, the solution appeared right in front of me while visiting a local restaurant. There on the table in Sutton's Berni Inn was a plastic holder with an insert card describing their range of liqueur coffees. I had decided on a Calypso before the penny dropped. These holders were exactly what we needed on each patient's bedside tables. Sadly, not to enable them to order an Irish coffee but to advertise Radio Marsden's programme schedule. I tracked down a supplier of the holders and, once I had explained their intended purpose, they gave us a good discount. A local printer produced the insert cards and off we went, visiting all the wards, to place one of our smart new programme guides on each patient's bedside unit. I can't recall if I actually asked the hospital management for permission to do this, and you certainly wouldn't get away without applying for that now. Happily, nobody objected and they were very successful. In addition to prompting patients to tune-in to our programmes, they also proved to be a great conversation subject with their visitors who tended to pick them up to read them. We all know how hard it can be to keep a conversation going when visiting someone in hospital and being able to discuss our programme holder and chat to the patient as to what it was all about gave them something else to say and could well have been the reason none of the ward staff or cleaners ever binned them!

We also had some large posters advertising our programmes printed. This time I definitely recall asking the hospital administrator for permission to put them up. One of these even appeared in a film scene, but you would have to be quick to spot it as it was on screen for a couple of seconds as the camera panned across to a bed. The film was *Champions,* made in 1984, telling the true story of jump jockey, Bob Champion who had made a full recovery from testicular cancer following treatment in The Royal Marsden. He then beat all the odds to go on to win the Grand National on Aldaniti. Having our poster in the film came about from a call I received from one of the film's set dressers who explained they were recreating one of The Royal Marsden's wards in a disused hospital and did I have some Radio Marsden posters they could use. I agreed to take them over to the film location, hoping I might be offered a part as an extra. I could see myself sauntering up to a bed and saying, 'Record request for you tonight Bob? Any racing tips for tomorrow?' That was not to be, as when I got there to hand over the posters they were still building the set. It was still exciting at least to have a glimpse behind the scenes and to be a very small part of the film process by way of being a props supplier. Sadly, much to my disappointment, Radio Marsden did not appear in the film credits.

Andrew Robertson works his magic on some of Radio Marsden's early studio equipment.

Our first major studio upgrade with its new layout and mixing desk. Only my Sony TC200 remains from Radio Marsden's early days.

Martin Ashton takes to the controls in the upgraded studio.

Phil Boys chooses a music track for his weekly Nightcap *programme.*

Andrew Perkins gets some hands-on experience of the new mixer.

Arthur Smith grabs yet another glass of water while driving the mixing desk.

Keith Warner preparing his programme. In my opinion, the best voice heard on Radio Marsden.

Alan Hart – Presenter and founder of our drama workshop, created a number of radio documentaries and comedy programmes.

James Pringle went from Radio Marsden to become a professional producer and programme presenter at Liverpool's Radio City. Now retired, he is pictured here at Academy FM Thanet where he hosts a three-hour weekend programme with his wife Mary.

Derek Power takes to the microphone as my co-presenter on 'Monday-go-Round'.

Part of our extensive library of LPs. It was some years before we tackled putting them on computer, so it was down to having a good memory to find that elusive Jim Reeves request!

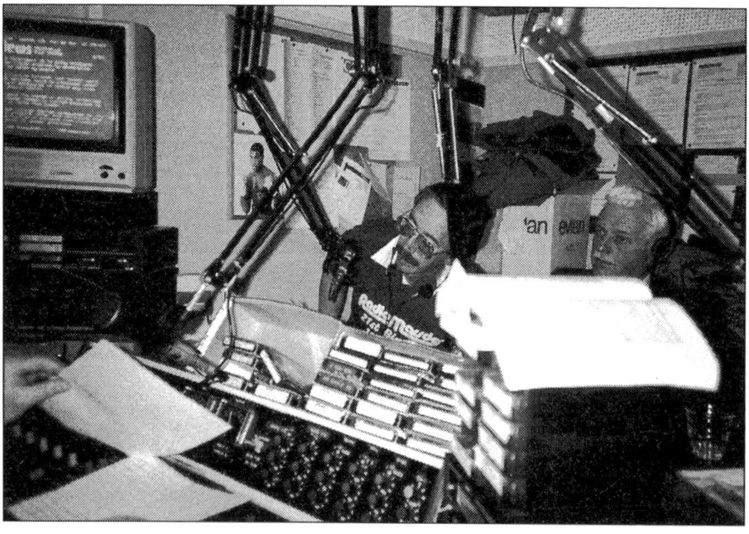

The second upgrade featured another new studio mixer, this one to broadcasting standards. We also installed cartridge machines to play in programme trails and station idents.

To make our programmes sound more professional, lots of notes became a necessity.

MONDAY-GO-ROUND
RUNNING ORDER

1.	INTRODUCTION	26.	RECORD INTRO.
2.	NEW PATIENTS (SUTTON)	27.	RECORD
3.	RECORD INTRO.	28.	BACK ANNOUNCE
4.	RECORD	29.	TAKE IT EAST TRAILER
5.	BACK ANNOUNCE	30.	HIT PARADE OF THE PAST
6.	SERVICES	31.	RECORD (HPP)
7.	COMEDY	32.	SERVICES
8.	SHOWCASE TRAILER	33.	QUICK QUIZ
9.	NEWSBREAK/COMMENT	34.	WED.N/CAP TRAILER
10.	RECORD INTRO.	35.	RECORD INTRO
11.	RECORD	36.	RECORD
12.	BACK ANNOUNCE	37.	BACK ANNOUNCE
13.	SERVICE	38.	TOP 5 BOOKS LIST
14.	CELEBRITY BIRTHDAYS	39.	SERVICES
15.	MONDAY N/CAP TRAILER	40.	STAFF AWARD
16.	NEWSBREAK/COMMENT	41.	NEWSBREAK/COMMENT
17.	RECORD INTRO.	42.	RECORD INTRO
18.	RECORD	43.	RECORD
19.	SERVICES	44.	BACK ANNOUNCE
20.	SUTTON N/P DRAW	45.	THURSDAY R.S. TRAILER
21.	STAFF CHOICE INTRO.	46.	TOP TEN RECORD LIST
22.	RECORD (STAFF CHOICE)	47.	RECORD (FROM TOP TEN)
23.	TUESDAY R.S. TRAILER	48.	PROG. OUTRO.
24.	INTRO.FULHAM ROAD	49.	
*25.	NEW PATIENTS (FULHAM	50.	

As did our running orders!

CHAPTER 5

Fundraising

I had initially used my own equipment, such as tape recorders and microphones, during the early days of presenting the request programme to the patients in the ward day room. The hospital was kind enough to cover the cost of building our first studio equipment necessary for us to actually broadcast, but we still needed funds to cover all sorts of other costs. Throughout my time at Radio Marsden, the Sutton League of Friends proved amazingly supportive and helped us right from the start with donations which regularly increased during my time there. A few years after I retired, Radio Marsden received a very substantial amount from them. Apparently, this money had been earmarked for a specialist piece of medical equipment, but the hospital decided at the last minute, they didn't require it after all, so the Sutton League of Friends donated it all to Radio Marsden. This enabled the station to invest in a new, state-of-the-art, computerised studio. One which would do justice to many local radio stations.

In addition to the League of Friends' help, we also organised our own fundraising. Once we started proper broadcasting, I registered Radio Marsden as a charity and from then on, produced annual accounts, kindly audited, free of charge, by the certified accountant I used for our business. Every year I sent off a set of the audited accounts to the Charity Commission, but in 22 years, I never received a reply with any queries or even an acknowledgement. The one document they sent was the certificate confirming our charitable status, apart from that, no communication at all. While I was happy with this and knew our accounts were in order, I did wonder if it was also the case for all other charities. An acknowledgement of having received the accounts would have at least given some confidence that there was somebody in the Charity Commission's office. It made me sceptical as to whether they were doing their job properly. With nearly 170,000 registered charities in England and Wales alone, they must have a large number of staff, but it is rare to read anything about the Commission taking any action against those not abiding by their strict regulations. While researching this book, I noticed some changes in the way the Charity Commission works, for example it now has an impressive online service. A click of the mouse brings up details of any charity searched and shows their income and whether their return is up to date or overdue. So, it seems improvements have been made!

One of our early fundraising ideas was to approach friends and family and offer them 'Associate Membership' of Radio Marsden. In return, they would receive a regular newsletter, a visit to our studio and a tour of the hospital (approval for which I don't recall asking the administrator for!). All these benefits came in return for the princely sum of £2 a year, an absolute bargain. We succeeded in signing up a good number of people, but running the scheme proved to be not cost effective. Failing to ask Associate Members to initially complete a bank standing order was a fundamental error. It meant we had to write to them again every 12 months, making the £2 donation very time-consuming to collect. The majority of donations were made possible by Radio Marsden's own members having fundraising contacts and convincing them we would be a worthy cause. Some of these were outstanding in giving their support and one couple, Kath and Eddie Gallacher, parents of one of our volunteers, raised over £3,000. This was shared between Radio Marsden and the Princess Chula Children's Ward. Our share enabled us to buy our first computer to improve finding a record in our ever-increasing collection of over 2,000 LPs and singles. The luxury of being able to type in the music request for the computer to immediately show you the relevant record's index number and location on the shelves was a dream come true. However, having the computer was one thing, inputting all the information to enable it to direct us to a record's location took well over a year and was a labour of love for the volunteers who undertook the task.

For many years we also took part in the annual Sutton Green Community Fayre by running their PA system on the day and raising some money for ourselves selling Radio Marsden mugs, pens and donated bric-a-brac. It was a rare opportunity for all of us to be together to promote the radio station. It was always a good day out, usually in the sunshine, despite the fact our team never won the Fayre's tug-of-war contest, not because we were lightweight, far from it, just not very good with rope.

Another successful fundraiser, although not for actual money, was to provide us with our own publication. We were approached by a company offering to give us, free of charge,

500 copies of an A5-size magazine. Half the content would be about Radio Marsden, featuring programme times, photos of presenters and general information about us. The remaining half would comprise advertisements from shops, restaurants and services close to the hospital. The publishing company paid the cost of producing the magazine and made the contacts with local businesses who would pay a fee to have their services advertised. Receiving the magazines without charge, enabled us to give every patient a copy and to have some left to hand out to interested visitors. A new edition was produced every year, so we were able to update its content with any changes to programmes and timings. We also did do an exercise to calculate how much we could make by doing it all ourselves, negotiating with the advertisers and finding someone to do the printing. We soon realised we could then have the 500 magazines as well as a few hundred pounds profit but sadly there were problems. It would require all the Radio Marsden volunteers to approach local businesses and sell them advertising space. That would involve daytime visits which, with us all having jobs, we would be unable to do. We settled for receiving the 500 free magazines and that arrangement continued for many years.

While benefiting a few times by obtaining a licence from the council to make a street collection in Sutton, the application process took ages with lots of paperwork involved. Each coin box had to be numbered and, after, the collection day, the donations had to be counted and bagged-up before making a special, pre-booked, visit to the bank to pay it in. A licence was only given every few years, as Sutton Council were inundated with similar requests from other charities, so opportunities to 'rattle boxes', which you're not actually allowed to do, were few and far between. A better solution came from one of our volunteers who knew the manager of Boots the Chemists, whose store enjoyed a prominent position in Sutton High Street. He offered Radio Marsden the use of their frontage between the pavement and his store which had plenty of room to set up a sound system. We could play music interspersed with some programme excerpts and some live interviews, while handing out Radio Marsden pens and balloons to promote the station. Best of all, we could legally shake our collecting tins as loud as we liked to invite donations as we were on the store's property rather than standing in the actual street. This proved to be a very lucrative fundraising event. Not only were we free to promote Radio Marsden but many people came up to us having either been a patient themselves or knowing a relative of friend who had received or was undergoing treatment. All of them had only kind words to say about The Royal Marsden and we were always amazed as to how many of the people we spoke to had some connection with the hospital. Such affection for The Royal Marsden reflected well on us and definitely boosted the amounts people put in our collection boxes. In some cases, when cashing up, we would find they contained a good number of £10 and £20 notes. The Sutton branch of Boots the Chemist supported Radio Marsden for many years, and we all enjoyed taking part in the day to promote the station and to give our finances a much-needed boost.

Following the success of the inaugural London Marathon in which runners raise large amounts for their selected charities, Radio Marsden decided it was time to do something similar. While most of us had by then given up smoking, we were certainly not natural athletes and rather than run, we thought walking would be more convivial and a lot less strenuous on our lungs and legs. A good number of volunteers signed up sponsors and a 20-mile route was plotted, starting and finishing at the hospital in Sutton. Walking this distance with very little training for most of us proved a fair challenge and, despite torrential rain on the day, we all completed it and, once the soreness in our legs had gone away, agreed it had been a very sociable way of raising money. The following year we took on the full marathon distance of 26 miles and 385 yards, and everyone agreed it was those final few yards that proved the most enjoyable. Interviews were conducted with the walkers along the route and Radio Marsden was on hand with a commentary as finishers hobbled down the entrance road to the hospital before finally collapsing in the car park.

Years later, Radio Marsden was also involved in the very successful Marsden March which first started in 2010 to raise funds to build the Oak Cancer Centre at Sutton. The route for this walk was between the two Royal Marsden hospitals with participants having a choice of distances. Radio Marsden provided eight hours of live coverage as up to 5,000 walkers trekked their way between the locations, providing them with much needed encouragement on the day as well as having some of its own volunteers taking part.

Our first Radio Marsden magazine.

Another unsuccessful attempt by Radio Marsden's tug-of-war team to win the annual competition at Sutton's Green Fayre.

Kath Gallacher presents the proceeds of her fundraising to Radio Marsden volunteer Liz, who also happened to be her daughter.

Fundraisers on duty on Sutton High Street. John Bridger, me, my wife Diana and our 2-year-old daughter Francesca, Radio Marsden's youngest volunteer.

CHAPTER 6

The Christmas shows

Our outside broadcast programmes from the wards soon became more complicated, sometimes having to run our wiring to up to three different locations for a quiz programme with patients on different wards pitting their wits against each other. The extra technical requirements soon saw me regularly endangering, maybe not my life, but certainly my ankles when making those perilous window drops to feed the cables down to the studio. Why was I not surprised when Andrew excitedly announced his grandest idea yet, nothing less than a Christmas show performed live in Pinkham Ward and simultaneously broadcast round the rest of the hospital. This would be a big undertaking with that ward chosen because it had the largest lounge area in the hospital with plenty of room to put on such an event.

Putting on such a show in front of an audience of patients and broadcasting it simultaneously sounded a great idea and exactly what Radio Marsden should be doing. We floated the idea to the hospital management, and they confirmed we could go ahead. Pinkham Ward was on the third floor of the building, so the lengths of cabling needed to send the programme down to our studio far exceeded the amounts we had. Fortunately, we were able to buy a couple of 100m drums of coax cabling thanks to the generosity of an extra donation made by our League of Friends to cover the costs of our first live Christmas show.

Having solved most of the technical issues, our thoughts turned to how we could entice entertainers to come to Sutton to perform in the show, at a time which for many was their busiest of the year. None of us had any showbusiness contacts, but Andrew, being at the BBC, reckoned he could ask Felix Bowness, their regular studio audience warm-up man. Felix agreed to come and perform but we were still a long way away from having any other acts. With the clock ticking down in early December and still no other performers in sight, I decided to contact *The Stage*, the weekly newspaper covering the entertainment industry. They agreed to publish a short article about our plea for entertainers and it brought an immediate response. While not being overwhelmed with offers from performers, three or four acts got in contact, which was a great result. We gratefully accepted all the artists who responded and at last we had enough acts to put on the show.

Andrew volunteered to be the MC which I was pleased about as my own abilities never went beyond radio. All the hospital staff were fantastic in giving up their time to support the show. The catering department provided food and a special cake. The ward staff helped rearrange the layout of the lounge and brought in extra chairs to accommodate as many patients as possible. Numerous other people, as well as the Radio Marsden teams, put in many extra hours planning every aspect of this special evening. One of our acts came to us, not from the appeal in *The Stage*, but through one of our own members who suddenly remembered her local greengrocer had theatrical contacts! That led to us being put in touch with Bob Curtiss, a professional comedian. Bob turned out to be a great supporter of Radio Marsden and came along to perform for us for a number of years. He once told me how he found our Radio Marsden Christmas show the hardest of the year to do. I asked him why that was, thinking maybe he had someone in his family suffering from cancer or had found it difficult performing to an audience mainly comprised of hospital patients. I got both of those wrong, it was nothing like that. Bob said, 'Thing is David, I earn my living as a comedian performing at stag and hen nights, so my act is full of very blue and risqué jokes. I don't usually do hospital audiences, so I really have to concentrate on keeping my act clean when I come along to do your Christmas show.' Bob always went down a storm with the patients, even cleaned-up, many of his jokes were near the knuckle and sometimes I wondered how he would have been received had we released the censorship handcuffs and asked him to give us one of his usual routines. I had a strong suspicion the audience would have loved it even more, but I never dared to take the risk. These were the days of prime-time TV shows such as *Till Death us Do Part* and *Love thy Neighbour* and compared to those, Bob's 20-minute act at The Royal Marsden was almost saintly. It also happened that another group of performers in that first Christmas show, was a choir from Croydon's Coloma Convent School, so probably it was just as well he reined in his act for us. His professional success grew in the 1970s and stretched to over 40 years, with him often appearing in cabaret as well as branching out to do after-dinner speaking and cruise work. His perfect comic timing led him to be described by his fellow professionals as *'the comedians' comedian'.*

Another of the entertainers who contacted us from our appeal in *The Stage* was Nadine Dubarry. This very glamorous lady styled herself as 'The French Singer from Paris' although at that time she resided in South London. Nadine explained in advance how her act consisted of a mixture of French and English songs with lots of audience participation. The fact she brought along her own backing track tape made it easy for us as she only needed one microphone. However, on the night, we suddenly got very worried when she asked to talk through her 'finale' requirements with the person in charge of our lighting board. Our problem was, we didn't actually have a lighting board as such, let alone an experienced person to operate one, just one of our volunteers looking after a couple of stage lights which could be turned either 'on' or 'off'. We all listened intently as Nadine told us she would leave the stage after her last song and our – newly appointed – lighting engineer must immediately fade-out, or in Radio Marsden's language, 'turn-off' the stage lights and time 10 seconds before turning them on again. She would then return to the stage to an expected, prolonged applause to perform a final number. It really worried us as to whether we could rely on our audience to clap for as long as 10 seconds to support Nadine's impromptu encore. As if this was not enough to give us the jitters, worse was to follow when an ashen-faced Andrew rushed up to me exclaiming, 'Guess what Nadine has just told me? There is one part of her act when she goes around pinning French things on the men in the audience!' This sounded seriously disturbing as we feared the obvious but, after consulting with her to seek some clarification, the 'things' turned out to be a kind of French flower. Come the show, we managed to get the lights off and on as instructed and our audience didn't let us down with their enthusiastic clapping for her encore. Nadine was a great hit, particularly unsurprisingly, mostly with our male patients who had kept hold of their French flowers as souvenirs. Not all our Christmas acts proved entirely suitable for the version of the show broadcast to the bedbound patients on other wards who were unable to come along to the party. While comedians, folk groups and a sing-along pianist were perfect for them, we also had a 'quick on the draw cartoonist' act. Although visually excellent on stage in the Pinkham Ward lounge, it didn't come across as being very entertaining to those listening on their headphones. Fortunately, we didn't have a magician performing which would have compounded that problem.

Over the next few years we continued with the Pinkham Ward Christmas shows. One of the highlights in 1974 was the guest appearance of two bunny girls from London's Playboy Club. Sandra and Janet stunned their audience, with their costumes complete with black velvet ears and fluffy white tails (it was different times back then). They also toured the hospital wards with trays of champagne, so everyone got a drink as well as the chance to meet them. Another year, we were fortunate to have one celebrity take part who lived literally 'round the corner'. This was Windsor Davies, a Welsh actor best known for his part as Battery Sergeant Major Williams in what has come to be perceived as the inappropriate TV sitcom, *It Ain't Half Hot Mum*. We thought his appearance would work best if he became the show's 'surprise guest'. That year we had some younger patients among the audience and decided to feature a version of ITV's popular *Who Do You*

Do? comedy impressions show.

We picked about six volunteers from the audience who happily came out to the front to try their hand doing impressions. The rounds proceeded until we were down to one young patient. For him to win whatever our star prize was, I asked him if he could finally impersonate Windsor's Sergeant Major character, whose memorable lines included, 'Mr La-di-da Gunner Graham', 'Shut up!' and 'Right, lovely boys, move yourselves'. The young lad made a brilliant job of those but was visibly shocked to then hear the booming tones of *'Shut up'* coming from behind the stage curtain before the 'real' Sergeant Major, Windsor Davies stepped forward to thunderous cheers and applause. It was a real surprise to everyone but particularly to our young winner. Thankfully, it didn't seem to affect him, in fact, just the opposite when you saw the wide grin on his face a few seconds later as Windsor warmly shook his hand and handed him his prize.

Our annual Pinkham Ward Christmas show continued to be well supported for a number of years with its mix of professional and local amateur performers. One year we welcomed another well-known celebrity guest in the form of actress Jan Francis who, at that time, starred alongside Paul Nicholas in the long-running BBC TV sitcom *Just Good Friends.* As time went on, we became a lot better technically at producing the event, even more so when one of our new volunteers suggested to his BBC boss that one of our shows would make a good training project for some of their apprentices. This was agreed and the BBC team arrived with a large van, jam- packed with professional broadcasting equipment. Three apprentices and their manager spent the day wiring it all in. When it came to transmit the show, the sound quality was a great improvement on our earlier efforts. However, what they had created proved a little too complicated for many of us Radio Marsden volunteers, as it included a number of facilities which would have been excellent if we had been professionals ourselves, but trying to operate their complicated talk-back system resulted in us not being as comfortable as we had been with our old methods of communicating between the ward and studio. To say those were basic would be an understatement. One year, the Christmas show's MC received his start and stop signals from another volunteer who waved a table tennis bat in his direction to signal when he should start and stop speaking!

In 1987, following changes to the lounge, Pinkham Ward became too small to use as a location. So, with no other suitable venue available in the hospital, it was back to the studio with each evening's team broadcasting their own special show in the week leading up to Christmas. I was one of the *Monday-Go-Round* team and decided to try and see if I could interview some of the professional actors performing in plays and shows in and around London, so off went more letters. I was surprised when the actor Norman Wisdom and his co-star, the actress and model Linda Lusardi, agreed to talk to me just before they took to the stage to perform in the pantomime *Cinderella* at Dartford's Orchard Theatre. Another performer who granted me a live interview was actor Andrew Cruickshank, best remembered for his role as Dr Cameron in the long-running BBC television series *Doctor Finlay's Casebook*. Andrew was playing the part of Justice Treadwell in the play *Beyond Reasonable Doubt* at London's Queens Theatre and spoke to me from his dressing room. He explained how his part required him to be on stage for the first scene but then not again until the last one. This meant he had to remain in his dressing room throughout the performance of most of the play. I'm not sure whether this Scottish actor might have whiled away the waiting time with a 'wee dram or two' but, when it came to give me his Christmas message for the patients, Andrew said how he much admired the treatment at The Royal Marsden Hospital as 'I have been in medicine himself'. I checked that fact after our interview, thinking, maybe he had been in the medical profession before starting his acting career. I could find nothing about that, so it seemed it must have referred to his time playing his television character in *Doctor Finlay's Casebook!*

The following year we decided to emulate our previous success, so off went more letters to various actors appearing in London theatres and once more received a good number of positive replies. Our 1988 *Monday-go-Round Christmas Show* went on air at 7pm and straight into a live interview with legendary singer, turned actor, Adam Faith who was starring, alongside BBC TV's *EastEnders* star Anita Dobson, in the musical version of *Budgie* at the Cambridge Theatre. It was just a few minutes before curtain-up and Adam would take to the stage, but he sounded very calm as he spoke from his dressing room about the pressure of doing the show. He was also enjoying an additional career as an investor and financial adviser. This involved him in calls and business meetings during the day which often continued late into the night. Adam was also writing weekly money advice columns for the *Daily Mail* and *The Mail on Sunday*, so all this extra work meant he usually didn't get to bed until the early hours of the morning. I thought that was impressive for someone who had, in recent years, undergone open heart surgery but had clearly decided not to take life easy. Talking about his Christmas plans, Adam said every Christmas Eve he arranged for a silver band to come to his house and play carols, which sounded rather awe-inspiring. When the interview drew to a close, I thanked him for his time and was staggered by his reply, 'That's alright, phone anytime!' A little later in our programme I played the interview I had recorded earlier with his co-star Anita Dobson. I was surprised by her warm and friendly voice, which was not a bit like that of Angie, the notorious character she played in BBC TV's *EastEnders*. Anita talked about the problems of trying to do her Christmas shopping as her face was so well known to the public that many would stop her in shops for a chat, treating her as a friend, rather than an actor. Anita said she was fine with them doing that, but it meant her shopping always took a lot longer to complete than she planned.

Our next call was with Colin Baker, an actor probably best known for being the sixth Doctor in the BBC TV's *Doctor Who*. At the time of my interview, Colin was about to go on stage at the Criterion Theatre in the comedy play *Run for your Wife*, which had run for over five years with more than 2,000 performances. Colin explained it was his first acting role in a farce, having only previously appeared on stage in a thriller called *Court*. He said he and his fellow actors were not allowed to ad lib by order of the writer and director Ray Cooney who would regularly drop in to watch a performance before issuing notes to the cast with recommendations which always concluded with the line 'there is always room for improvement'. Colin was followed by a quick chat with fellow actor Bill Pertwee. I asked Bill, best known for his part as Chief ARP Warden Hodges in BBC's sitcom *Dad's Army*, how he relaxed once the curtain came down? I was very amused by his succinct reply: 'a scotch and a bath bun.'

Following on from Colin and Bill, the programme's next destination was London's Aldwych Theatre to interview a very amicable Timothy West who was starring in *The Sneeze*, a play by Michael Frayn, based on four of Anton Chekhov's plays. I said this sounded a rather serious play to put on around Christmas, but Timothy quickly corrected me, saying how Chekhov actually wrote good comedy and the play contained many funny lines. I asked him what it was like working alongside the play's co-star Rowan Atkinson, best known at that time for his part as Edmund in the long-running BBC series *Blackadder*, as it was a few years before the debut of his, even more successful character, the bumbling Mr Bean. Timothy said he got along with him very well and, like most comedy actors, Rowan was actually a very serious person in real life. Timothy's usual end-of-show routine was to leave the theatre and stroll over Waterloo Bridge to meet his wife. She was actress Prunella Scales, then appearing at the National Theatre, and they would then drive home to Berkshire, finally getting to bed around 1 am. Away from the theatre, their relaxation was their ownership of a canal boat. I am sure he could not have imagined that 15 years later, this pastime would lead himself and Pru to star in the successful Channel 4 series *Great Canal Journeys.*

We rounded up that year's Christmas show with two more interviews. The first with actress Maureen Lipman, starring at London's Fortune Theatre in her one-woman show *Re:Joyce!* a celebration of the work of comedienne Joyce Grenfell. I told Maureen that following our interview, we would be playing the famous Joyce Grenfell song 'Stately As A Galleon' and she expressed disappointment at that, saying she preferred Joyce's more poignant songs and monologues, such as 'First Flight', about a lady flying to America to meet her family, and 'Boat Train', about a woman seeing her family off as they emigrated. Maureen explained how Joyce had written more serious dialogues as she got older, although her early comedy songs had remained the most popular with her fans. With *Re:Joyce!* being a one-woman show, Maureen found it very tiring, especially on days with two performances, so she usually went straight home at the end of the evening, in her own words 'to collapse'. When I asked Maureen how she was getting on with her Christmas shopping she said she had been in a shop in Covent Garden that afternoon and picked up a waistcoat she liked before asking a shop assistant if he had that size in the blue. His reply was, 'Yes, in the blue, the yellow and the red, in all the sizes.' She had laughed at that as it was one of the frequent drawbacks of her starring in the highly popular series of British Telecom advertisements at the time. One of these featured her character, Beattie, on the telephone to a shop assistant, played in the advertisement by actor Richard Wilson, constantly asking him to look on the rack to see if he had in stock a particular colour or size of a blouse she liked. It ended with her character saying, 'So, you have all the colours in both the sizes, you haven't sold out of anything?' 'No,' replies the, by now extremely harassed Richard, to which Maureen replies, 'It's not what you would call all the rage is it?' Hence the Covent Garden shop assistant's reply to her innocent enquiry earlier in the day.

My final interview for that year's Christmas show was with the 'king of farce' himself, the recently knighted, Sir Brian Rix who had just returned to the stage to star in the play *Dry*

Rot at the Lyric Theatre. I asked him how difficult he had found the return to acting, having previously retired to take up a role in a production company, as well as his voluntary work as chairman of the charity Mencap. Brian said his return had been very evocative, but it was also tiring being back on the acting treadmill once again, after his previous 12,000 performances spanning 30 years. Brian was enjoying the play which also starred his wife Elspeth Grey. Once the run was over, he would be busy with the book launch of *Farce about Face*, the second part of his autobiography, which he hoped would be as successful as his first volume, *My Farce from my Elbow.*

One of our patient handouts advertising a Pinkham Ward Christmas party.

Comedian Bob Curtiss gets the Christmas show off to a great start.

Local folk group Tamarin entertain with their music.

Country singer Jane Sullivan entertains the patients.

MC Keith Warner introduces TV's Just Good Friends *actress, Jan Francis to the audience.*

CHAPTER 7

Star interviews

There were only a small number of celebrities who could spare the time to make an evening visit to the hospital, so the majority who responded to our letters agreed to be interviewed at a location more convenient to them. These ranged from their own homes, their agent's office or somewhere far more exciting, their place of work. That could be the BBC's Broadcasting House or Television Centre, a London theatre, or best of all, on a film set. I have selected the following interviews because I hope they will prove the most interesting due to their content and sometimes their location.

SPIKE MILLIGAN – Writer, comedian, actor and musician

I was very excited to receive a call from Norma Farnes, Spike Milligan's agent and manager, to tell me he had agreed to an interview at his office in London's Bayswater. I arrived on the due day and was shown into a large room which looked more like a bedsit. The first thing to catch my eye was a half-built upright piano sitting among a host of other crazy items of furniture. I asked Spike if this really was just his office and he said he also slept here during weekdays and returned to his actual home for weekends.

Spike Milligan was the multi-talented, exceedingly eccentric co-creator of *The Goon Show* and a much-loved and respected comic, author and actor of his time. His parents named him Terence, but he had been nicknamed Spike during his army days and adopted it as he liked Spike Jones and his City Slickers, a band he used to listen to on Radio Luxembourg. I began the interview and Spike said he never planned to be a comedian or writer, as first and foremost he considered himself a musician. His first paid engagement had been playing guitar in the Harlem Club Dance Band for which he received seven shillings for a performance in Brockley, South East London. He was called-up and served in the army during the Second World War. When I interviewed him, thanks to his prodigious diary keeping, his first autobiographical account of those years, *Adolf Hitler: My Part in His Downfall*, had just been published to great critical acclaim and he was to go on to produce a further six volumes covering his time in the army. Sometime after being demobbed, Spike decided to concentrate on writing comedy. He had met Harry Secombe during his army years, and a mutual chemistry had developed between them. That led to contact with two other like-minded comedians, Peter Sellers and Michael Bentine. The four of them formed the group who went on to write, produce and star in *The Goon Show*, arguably the most famous radio series of all time, keeping the nation laughing through over 200 episodes between 1950 and 1960.

I asked Spike which gave him the most satisfaction to work in, stage, radio or television? His reply was very clear, 'Stage for fulfilment, radio for imagination and TV for the money.'

He had also made a few films which he described as 'a load of crap' except for *The Running, Jumping & Standing Still* which he made in 1959. This 11-minute short was filmed in a field with Peter Sellers and its production costs were £100. It had even been good enough to have received a nomination for an Academy Award. Spike expressed his annoyance that, despite the film being his idea, Sellers and his co-producer Dick Lester seemed to have received all the plaudits.

Spike said he was very interested in politics and was clearly an environmentalist well ahead of his time. He was against vivisection, factory farming and over development. He explained how we couldn't go on at the rate we were building airports everywhere without us ending up with serious pollution problems. Having finished the interview, as was my custom, I asked Spike if he could record a get-well message for the patients. He readily agreed but what followed was nothing less than a ten-minute tirade. It started off well with, 'I hope all of you will soon be better' but he went on, asking the listening patients to use the fact they were in The Royal Marsden Hospital suffering from cancer, to put pressure on their MP and any other contacts they had, to back his idea to reduce the number of cases of lung cancer. He explained he had been in contact with a medical professor who was backing his campaign to change the content of cigarettes. His suggestion was for them to be two-thirds filter and just one-third tobacco. I could not fault the idea, but it was a bit extreme for a 'get-well message' we planned to drop into our programmes. When he finished and I had turned off the tape recorder, he looked me in the eye and with great passion said, 'You will play that to the patients, won't you?' I had to lie, replying 'Of course we will Spike' before making my exit. For such a big star, he was very easy to interview. A very sensitive and fragile man, Spike Milligan had already entertained millions through his TV comedy and many writings and would go on to do so until his death in 2002. Ever the comedian, even his gravestone brings a smile to all who see it as it bore the self-penned epitaph; *I told you I was ill.*

ANDREW GARDENER – ITN Newscaster

Graham and I travelled to London's ITN studios to interview Andrew, one of the original presenters of *News at Ten*. Our first and overwhelming impression on meeting him was his height, at least 6'5". His earliest TV appearance had been in 1961 on a BBC TV pilot programme called *Table Talk*. It was a lunchtime broadcast and centred around guests conversing about pre-planned subjects. He said he was petrified the first time he presented it as the guests actually ate lunch in the studio and the programme would be broadcast live from when coffee was served following the meal. Andrew said that it had been easy to think you were in an actual restaurant rather than a studio. He also told a funny story of how the BBC had sent him out to interview a man who said he had invented shoes to enable a person to walk on water. He met the inventor at the Regent's Canal to record a feature with him and to try them out. Having put on the shoes, Andrew had a ski pole in one hand and his microphone in the other. A colleague held the valuable tape recorder and stayed safely on the towpath as Andrew eased himself onto the canal to do a commentary as he tried to walk on the water. He reckoned he lasted less than ten seconds before falling in headfirst.

I asked him about being a newsreader on *News at Ten* and

he picked me up immediately on his job description. He was adamant he was a newscaster. He explained the difference being he was involved in the preparation of the programme as part of the team and not just reading the scripted news. He considered the tip of the iceberg was the actual screening of the 30-minute news programme as all the real work was done during the many hours leading up to then. The programme's closing scene always featured the two newscasters turning to each other for a chat as the theme tune played and the credits rolled over the screen. Hoping to discover what some of those short conversations might be about, I asked Andrew what was said between himself and the other newscaster during that final scene. He replied it was a state secret and he would be out of a job if he told me. It was better than the 'If I told you I'd have to kill you' reply I was expecting, and it showed what a real gentleman he was. He even took us on a tour of the studio and onto the *News at Ten* set to sit behind the famous news desk. Just as you would expect, he was a very smooth talker. Until that is, the moment arrived to record the usual 'get-well message' I asked for at the end of the interview. He kept getting in a muddle and fluffed his lines when it came to 'All of you listening to Radio Marsden in The Royal Marsden Hospital'. After a few unsuccessful attempts, he finally took out his pen and wrote his message down before proceeding to do a perfect take. Only to be expected I suppose from a newscaster who lived by the autocue.

CILLA BLACK – Singer and TV entertainer

Of all the celebrities I interviewed for Radio Marsden, Cilla stands out as the most talkative. In fact, it was hard to stop her and I became worried as to whether there would be enough tape on my machine to last our time together. She was very relaxed and friendly when we met in her agent's London office and that helped to put me at my ease in the company of such a big star. Her highly detailed and often humorous answers to my questions made my job very easy, which was not the case with all the celebrities I met. Cilla explained how, from a very early age, she always wanted to be a singer and would practise in the bathroom as a child. As a teenager she was influenced by the American rock and roll and blues singer Frankie Lymon and his group, the Teenagers. Cilla was 12 and Frankie 13 when she started to mimic him, and by the time she was 13, she said you couldn't tell the difference between them as they had the same type of voice. Cilla was soon singing around the clubs in her hometown of Liverpool and owed her career to John Lennon. He had heard her sing at the Cavern Club and told The Beatles manager Brian Epstein about her. Brian came along to hear her one night, but Cilla messed up that first audition. Thankfully, she got a second chance to sing in front of him and this time she nailed the audition and the rest, as they say, is history.

Starstruck as a child, Cilla spent a lot of her time chasing around for autographs of the popular singers of her time. These included stars such as Cliff Richard. By the time she too was famous and appearing in a Royal Command Performance, she was shocked when Cliff approached her after the show asking for her autograph. In Cilla's words, 'I went off him a bit after that but, on reflection, I thought it was very nice.' She told me *Alfie* was her favourite song but had only agreed to record it if its writer, Burt Bacharach, conducted the orchestra and was in the studio at the time. Cilla particularly enjoyed singing it in cabaret where she could best deliver its killer vocal. Away from work, her favourite pastime was watching TV. She also enjoyed golf but lacked the time to play very often. Her first son, Robert, had recently been born, so a lot of her time was now taken up with him. In 1968 she had starred in the Peter Hall-directed film *Work is a Four-Letter Word*. She was honest in admitting she had gone to see it three times but still didn't understand what it was all about. Despite this, she still harboured ambitions to be a film star but her career had already turned to television which was proving as great a success as her singing career. She was about to embark on her third TV series of *Cilla* which would go on to run for a further five years after our interview. Her success continued with the follow-up shows, *Blind Date* and *Surprise Surprise* and she remained a firm favourite with UK audiences right up to her unexpected sad death in 2015.

ROY HUDD – Comedian

I have earlier described Roy Hudd's visit to Radio Marsden and how entertaining he was. However, my first time of meeting him was in 1972 when Graham and I went to interview him in his dressing room at London's Palace Theatre. Roy was appearing in the hit show *Danny La Rue at the Palace*. Danny La Rue was an Irish entertainer known for wearing amazing dresses as most of his stage performances were in drag. The show featured music-hall-type bawdy sketches, with Danny wearing a vast array of expensive and, as the evening went on, ever more outrageous costumes.

Roy Hudd was the funniest men I ever interviewed. He even coped with my 'Do you have a favourite joke?' question which had been known to flummox a good few other comedians, sometime resulting in a long pause to think of one. To avoid this, I changed tactics and would alert them to the question in advance. Roy needed no such warning and had little hesitation in reeling off his current favourite: 'Politicians have been saying the same old things for years. Dear old Churchill said, "Give me the tools and I'll lead you to the Promised Land." Moses said, "Mount your ass and I will lead you to the Promised Land" and only last week at the TUC Conference, Vick Feather said, "Put down your tools, sit on your arses, this is the Promised Land." I'm not sure how much of those sayings were actually true but it was a good joke back in 1970 when Trade Unions were a lot stronger and newsworthy than they are now. When we met, Roy was in his twelfth year of showbusiness. He had left National Service in 1958 and become a Butlin's Redcoat. He had based his comedy style on the famous music hall performer Max Miller, and for three years he performed a double act with a friend before starting out on his solo career. He recounted how, in his days at Butlins, their act involved a lot of going off and coming back on stage after quick changes for different sketches and routines. One night, the pair rushed off for a costume change for their *Singing in the Rain* routine just as the backstage lights failed. Roy grabbed what he thought was his raincoat and ran back on stage, only to discover he was wearing a giant polythene bag!

Croydon born and bred, Roy had always been a Crystal Palace fan, having followed them for over twenty-five years. He reminisced about the players he had watched from the terraces, Fred and Albert, the Dawes brothers and Baldy Bassett, a player whose unlikely name brought the interview to a temporary halt as Graham and I dissolved into fits of laughter.

Roy talked about his passionate interest in old time music hall and how he was an avid collector of playbills and other memorabilia from those Victorian times. His own favourite comedians were Ken Dodd, Tommy Cooper and Frankie Howerd. He had got his first TV break appearing with David Frost in *Not So Much a Programme, More a Way of Life*. I asked how he got on with him. He laughed, saying, 'David Frost?' I saw him just this morning, walking to work across the Serpentine!' He went on to explain that, even after six months working together, David was still a very difficult man to get to know as he was a workaholic. Interestingly, these were similar comments I had heard about him from John Cleese. Sadly, I never got to interview David Frost. When we finished the interview, Roy asked if he could recite a monologue he had thoughtfully brought along as it was near to Christmas and he reckoned the patients could do with a little cheering up. It was wonderful, all about how families visit each other's houses, who does what and how it all gets a bit too much by the end of the festivities. We played it throughout December and the patients loved it. The fact he had taken time to think about our interview ahead of our visit impressed me a lot and said much about his character. He deserved all the success he went on to enjoy across all aspects of showbusiness in a career that would stretch to 60 years.

RONNIE CORBETT – Comedian

I interviewed comedian Ronnie Corbett on two separate occasions. The first at the BBC TV Centre where he had agreed to talk to me between takes of an episode of the highly successful *The Two Ronnies*. This series featured him and Ronnie Barker performing sketches, usually ending with a musical number mimicking one of the popular bands of the time. Corbett also had a feature in each show where he would sit in an oversize chair and spin-out a monologue, much to the amusement of the studio audience. Graham and I were shown into his dressing room and told to wait there as he was just in the middle of recording a sketch for the show. Sometime later, in walked Ronnie looking rather sullen and a little morose. This was the opposite to what I had expected, which was him bounding in cracking jokes. I mistakenly thought comedians were naturally always happy, just like Roy Hudd had been. Ronnie Corbett was definitely not happy that day. He lit up a small cigar, and before we started, I did my usual warm-up explaining about Radio Marsden and, of course, finished with raising that matter of the favourite joke question. Ronnie thought for a moment before replying, 'No, I don't think I have, you'd better leave that question out.' My first thought was he was turning the joke on me but soon realised by the look on his face that he wasn't. He was clearly in no mood for jokes. The tape recorder was switched on and I proceeded with the interview. To each of my questions he gave the bare minimum answer which taught me a lesson. I had been fortunate in having very easy people to talk to in previous interviews but this one was completely different. Ronnie was not cooperating, and we were all done and dusted in ten minutes before being immediately shown out of his dressing room. On the drive home, Graham and I discussed what had happened. Had I gone about the interview the wrong way, thinking he would have been as funny as Roy Hudd? We soon decided that was not the case and it was more likely there had been problems rehearsing the sketch he had been doing before returning to his dressing room and we were probably the last people he wanted to see just then. Maybe it had gone wrong for him and needed numerous takes. I later discovered a lot of the sketches were written by Ronnie Barker under the pseudonym Gerald Wiley. When you watched episodes of *The Two Ronnies*, many of their two-handed scenes had complicated dialogue requiring a lot of quick learning. Knowing and seeing some of those, now famous, sketches convinced me that on the day of our interview, Ronnie Corbett was suffering a difficult day at the studio and we had not met his real self.

A few years later I contacted his agent again and Ronnie agreed to do a live telephone interview from his home in Croydon. This time he was everything you would have expected from one of the country's most loved comedians and it restored my faith in him. That first experience was a good lesson in not expecting every comedian you meet to be funny; they all have immense pressure to deal with and it's easy to catch them on a bad day.

SIR STANLEY BAKER – Actor and film director

It was always exciting to receive a celebrity's positive response to one of our letters, and even better if the interviewee asked for it to be recorded in their home, as paying them a visit gave an insight as to how they lived away from the cameras. In the case of film actor and producer Stanley Baker, it couldn't have been better. He asked if we could meet him at his London base, which just happened to be a penthouse along the Albert Embankment, overlooking the Thames and the Houses of Parliament. We were shown into a vast lounge with its fabulous three-sided views looking out over the river. Graham and I were, naturally, completely awestruck.

His assistant told us 'Mr Baker will be with you shortly' before leaving us to wander around. The shelves were filled with set models from his many films, in particular *Zulu*, his most successful so far. After about ten minutes, Stanley strode in looking very much the actor and bearing a striking resemblance to Richard Burton. He settled easily into the interview and explained how he had begun in theatre aged 13 at school in the Rhondda Valley. He owed the beginning of his career to a matter of luck. A casting director from Ealing Studios, on a visit from London to South Wales, researching possible locations, happened to also be looking for a young boy to play a part in his new film. Stanley was appearing in his school's end-of-term play and, on seeing his performance, the director was sufficiently impressed to whisk him down to London to do a screen test which led to his first acting part in the film *Undercover.* That was followed by a role in the play *The Druid's Rest* at London's St Martin's Theatre, where the 14-year-old Stanley took to the stage alongside Richard Burton. He went on to learn the business of acting at Birmingham Rep and had numerous stage and film parts ever since. His major influence was a master from his school who saw something in him at an early age and encouraged Stanley to become an actor. That same teacher continued to take an interest in his career through the years and Stanley was still in regular touch with him whenever he felt he needed advice, even though he was now at the top of his profession. Despite his success as a film actor, Stanley said he preferred theatre because he found the audience response more satisfying as they immediately showed their appreciation, or sometimes, non-appreciation.

Making the film *Zulu* had given Stanley his most

satisfaction as it was the first he had produced as well as starred in. He was extremely busy with ongoing discussions for new films and parts, as well as being a founder and part-owner of Harlech Television based in his native Wales. With so many work interests, he admitted to finding it difficult to relax when not working. He was a devoted family man but, when time allowed, loved to play golf. Such was his love of the game that, given his life again, Stanley said he would have rather been a professional golfer. His proudest moments had been the births of his four children and attending the royal premiere of *Zulu*. He bemoaned the sorry state of the British film industry, brought on by the recession the country was experiencing at the time of our interview but said it should be seen as an opportunity to separate the wheat from the chaff by getting rid of the advantage-seeking producers. He predicted better times ahead for the industry as the flexibility of working hours and the production quality in the UK film studios far exceeded that found in Hollywood. He was against censorship but saw the current need for it and thought it would be better for the public to control it for themselves by not going to see the worst of the 'smutty' films, rather than being prohibited to see them by the British Board of Film Censors.

Stanley was in favour of cinemas being allowed to have more comfortable lounges and bar areas for the sale of alcohol, innovations that the cinema industry adopted a few years later. The fellow actors he most admired were Marlon Brando, Paul Schofield and Sir Laurence Olivier, who had chosen him early in his career to play the leading role in *Richard III*. In answer to my final question, as to whether he had any unfulfilled ambitions, he said how he just wanted to go on doing what he was doing as he didn't consider it as work, just pure enjoyment.

By the time Graham and I left his penthouse it was early evening. Parked outside the entrance to the building was an impressive chauffeur-driven black Rolls Royce. Stanley had asked us about The Royal Marsden and told us he lived in Epsom, just a few miles from the hospital. Was this his Rolls waiting to take him home we wondered? Surely it had to be, and we calculated if we waited long enough at the bus stop right outside the building, he was bound to spot us and take pity on a couple of hospital radio lads, resulting in Stanley giving us a lift in his limousine and dropping us off home. We discussed the logistics of this plan as both of us actually lived in Wallington, about five miles from Sutton. Should we receive a lift, it might be pushing our luck to ask Stanley's chauffeur to make such a long detour. Instead, we decided we would say we lived close by the hospital, in Sutton as that was on the route to Epsom. We could be dropped off there and make our way back to Wallington. The time involved would be well worth it for the experience of being driven by Rolls Royce, in the company of one of Britain's top film stars. We were agreed on our plan and continued to stand at the stop for almost an hour, refusing to board the next four buses before finally giving up and taking the fifth one. Had Stanley Baker been delayed in his flat? When we recounted the story to friends, most were quick to suggest an alternative reason for his no-show. Maybe he spent the time looking over his penthouse balcony and wishing those two chancers from hospital radio would get on a bus so he could leave his office and be driven home in peace. So cruel, but I'm prepared to give him the benefit of the doubt and put it down to a long telephone call with some Hollywood producer about his next film project. Sadly, Stanley Baker died in 1976 at the comparatively young age of 48. Shortly before his death, he was planning a follow-up film to *Zulu* and had been granted a knighthood in the Queen's New Year honours list. A well-deserved award, but one Sir Stanley was unable to receive in person, his death coming before his investiture.

HUGHIE GREEN – TV presenter

During the height of his TV fame in the 1960s and 70s, when he was hosting top-rated quiz and talent shows, Hughie Green was someone you either loved or hated. I met up with him in his flat above Baker Street tube station. He explained how he had always wanted to be in showbusiness and had his first big break at the age of 12 appearing on BBC radio's *In Town Tonight*, an early type of interview and entertainment show. There he met its presenter Eric Maschwitz. Hughie, confident at such a young age, had no hesitation in telling him the BBC needed 'a jolly good kids show'. Maschwitz told him told to go away and write one and come back when he had put it together, hoping that would be the last he saw of him. Instead, Hughie was back three days later, at Broadcasting House, along with a bunch of other kids, announcing 'I'm here ready for the audition'. That was the start of *Hughie Green and his Gang* which the BBC immediately broadcast. He explained how, by the time he was 15, around 250 people were involved performing and producing the show which went on to become a successful concert party, touring in both this country and Canada. This was followed by Hughie being offered his first film part, no less than the lead role in the 1935 production *Midshipman Easy.* I was slightly sceptical but had to believe him when he said he even got to choose, not only his director, Carol Reed, but also his leading lady, the then 19-year-old Margaret Lockwood.

Hughie returned to television to host the long-running talent show *Opportunity Knocks*, a forerunner of *Britain's Got Talent*, which was first broadcast on radio before, in 1956, transferring to television. *Opportunity Knocks* was responsible for discovering some of Britain's top acts including, Les Dawson, Little and Large, Frankie Vaughan, Mary Hopkin and The Batchelors. Hughie also presented the equally long-running quiz show *Double Your Money* and explained how he was constantly in a ratings war with another of ITV's quiz programmes, *Take Your Pick* which was hosted by Michael Miles. When I pressed him as to whether his continuous and well-publicised verbal sniping about Miles was genuine, Hughie admitted it was just friendly rivalry as, in real life, they were the best of friends. He described his hobbies, which were flying and model railways. Now I already knew about his love of model railways from my research and that he had a dedicated room for his extensive layout, right there in his Baker Street flat. I asked him about it and Hughie confirmed it was true, so I was then itching to see it. Sadly, he didn't invite me to the train room, and I didn't have the courage to ask, so I never got to see it, something I've regretted ever since. I found Hughie Green easy to talk to, a very sensitive man despite his TV persona of over confidence and he went out of his way to make the interview entertaining for the patients, by dropping in various comic references to hospital life. We finished with him recording a Christmas get-well message for the patients and I smiled as he managed to both start and end it with his famous catchphrase: 'and I mean that most sincerely folks.'

ROGER MOORE – Actor

Without doubt, Roger Moore was the biggest star I ever had the privilege to interview for Radio Marsden. I received a phone call in response to our letter. His agent apologised that Roger would be unable to come to Sutton, but would it be possible for me to go to Pinewood Studios in Buckinghamshire to record the interview on the set where he was filming *The Persuaders*, a new series for ITV. That sounded pretty exciting and obviously I had no hesitation in saying yes. I felt rather special driving up to Pinewood's iconic half-timbered mock Tudor entrance gate where I announced my appointment with one of the most famous actors in Britain. I was directed through to the visitors' car park and made my way to reception where I was checked-in before being escorted to the actual studio. There I was introduced to Roger's PA who explained how I would have to record the interview during the breaks between filming, when the crew reset the stage and make changes to camera and lighting positions. This was all very exciting and I could easily edit the interview back at the Radio Marsden studio. I assumed the actors went to their dressing rooms between shots, but instead they just moved off the set into various corners. The particular scene they were shooting that afternoon featured the two stars, Roger Moore and Tony Curtis, along with a guest appearance by Terry Thomas, also a much-loved British film star. I soon spotted Roger on the set, not only by his instantly recognisable face, but more so by his sartorial elegance which was in keeping with his part as the British aristocrat, Lord Brett Sinclair. When the first break in filming was called, I was taken over to a corner to meet Roger who was standing next to an artist's easel. He gave me a warm welcome before asking if I would like to see what he did to fill the time between takes. 'Yes please,' I replied, and he promptly flipped over a page of the large drawing pad to reveal a semi-pornographic drawing of a female form with flowers protruding from a rather personal area. I was shocked at seeing this but tried hard not to show it. Roger had a twinkle in his eye, and I did think it was a bit of a wind-up but as we started the interview, he told me how his first choice of profession had actually been to be an artist, hence the between-takes-hobby I had just witnessed. Roger explained how he had not been good enough for a career in art, so became an actor instead.

His first role was at the Arts Theatre in the Eugene Labiche's farce *The Italian Straw Hat* in which he had played a French gendarme. He said his mother came to see one of his performances, but his character had to wear an enormous eighteenth-century hat which came down to his nose, so she really didn't see anything of his face. The same problem occurred with his next part, a Chinese officer in Bertolt Brecht's play *The Caucasian Chalk Circle* in which he wore a large helmet with nose and earpieces. Again, his mother was unable to see his face. Roger was really running with this story now and told me there were further problems with his mother when she went to see him in the 1956 film *Diane*, in which his character Prince Henri wore an enormous crown. Still not finished with this tale, Roger went on to say his mother also said she failed to recognise him in one of his first major TV roles playing the 12th-century swashbuckling Ivanhoe. By now I had the distinct feeling he was pulling my leg as, the more this story went on, the wider became the smile across Roger's face. He finally ended his answer by saying his mother had also complained, after watching him play Simon Templar in TV's *The Saint*, saying she could only occasionally see his face when the halo wasn't across his eyes! By this time, I was sure I had been well and truly 'had', but when I later referenced all the characters he had mentioned, every one he had played was exactly as he had said.

Characterising his current role as Lord Brett Sinclair, alongside Tony Curtis as the self-made American Danny Wilde, Roger defined *The Persuaders* as an action-adventure series and likened it to a modern-day version of Laurel and Hardy. This was made even more believable as they had been joined on set that day by the comedian and character actor Terry Thomas, himself a star of such films as *School for Scoundrels* and *It's a Mad, Mad, Mad, Mad World*. I moved on to ask Roger Moore about the part which had resulted in his worldwide stardom, that of Simon Templar in ITV's *The Saint*. Roger played the famous investigator in over 100 episodes and explained how, before he even got the part, he had tried to buy the TV rights to *The Saint* books from their author Leslie Charteris, but Leslie had refused to sell them to him. A short while later he had a call from ITV's Lew Grade asking if he wanted the part of Simon Templar in the new series. He had vowed not to do another long-running TV character but immediately said yes, thinking it would only run for six months. Instead, 118 episodes were broadcast over seven years, making Roger Moore a household name. Its success was helped by Roger's ability to raise one eyebrow, an action that became Simon Templar's trademark. Roger said he physically resembled Templar but certainly not in character. He pulled no punches explaining how *The Saint* was basically a fascist who poked his nose into other people's business and interfered with the police in the performance of their duties and he was not like that at all. Roger had directed some episodes of *The Saint*, and had enjoyed doing so, as it meant he had no director to argue with!

Roger said how he would have loved to have taken on the role of *James Bond* before it was given to Sean Connery and how the film producer Harry Saltzman actually offered it to him later, when Sean was considering not playing the part again, but by then Roger had committed to his current role in *The Persuaders*. I failed to realise at the time of the interview, that this could have been my first Radio Marsden scoop as Roger <u>did</u> finally become the famous James Bond agent 007 a little over 12 months after our meeting at Pinewood. When I asked him which of his many acting roles had given him the most satisfaction, he said it had been his recent role in the Basil Dearden-directed film, *The Man Who Haunted Himself.* Roger had played the highly emotional lead character, Harold Pelham, who was taken over by some kind of spirit while driving along the M4, forcing him to crash the car. In the film, Pelham was at one point clinically dead on the operating table. Roger went on to tell me that, in a tragic coincidence, shortly after the film was released, Basil Dearden was driving along the M4 having left the film studios and was killed when he lost control of the car after hitting a traffic sign. All very spooky indeed.

Roger's hectic work commitments and young family gave him little time for hobbies, but he liked tennis, swimming, poker and also the guitar, which he admitted he played badly. Unlike most superstars, he actually enjoyed being spotted in the street, although there were times when it could be invasive. He said he would be slightly offended if he were not recognised, as his celebrity status could always be relied upon to help him secure a table in any top restaurant, no matter how full it was. He enjoyed the travelling his work entailed and was an advocate of making English a one-world language to improve understanding between nations. He reckoned it had worked well with the US and the British Commonwealth, so why not extend it to all other nations to improve communications? Roger also expressed an interest in politics but was not actively involved in any one party. Finally, he told me he had an unfulfilled ambition to direct a full-length feature film.

After our interview, Roger invited me to stay and watch the filming which I did until late in the afternoon when it finished for the day. I admit I was itching to ask Roger if Tony Curtis would mind recording a few words for Radio Marsden but thought it would be disrespectful to him as he had given me so much of his own time. I later read an article which said the two of them didn't get on during the filming of *The Persuaders* as Tony Curtis was always keen to leave the studio as early as he could, whereas Roger was happy to extend his working day if the crew required it. I thoroughly enjoyed just standing around watching it all happen, knowing I was very privileged to be allowed to be there to see how a TV series was filmed. There were so many technical interruptions that only one scene was filmed that afternoon. Little do we appreciate the immense amount of time and effort that goes into the making of what we see on the TV or watch in the cinema.

I finally left Pinewood late afternoon and drove home. Despite the rush-hour traffic jams, I had a smile on my face and couldn't help looking across at other motorists and thinking, 'I bet they've not been interviewing Roger Moore at Pinewood Studios this afternoon.' I was very proud to have been invited there to meet such a personable and warm-natured man. I am not surprised he went on to become a UNICEF Goodwill Ambassador and remained a truly big star until his death in 2017.

KEVIN KEEGAN AND THE ENGLAND FOOTBALL TEAM

Not many hospital radio stations can boast of having an England football captain as its own roving reporter aboard a coach taking his team to Wembley to play an international match, but that's what happened when Kevin Keegan did exactly that. I had sent letters and a cassette tape out to various London football clubs, asking if some of their players could record get-well messages for our patients. There had been absolutely no response, until a couple of months later when an envelope arrived containing a tape and a note from Fred Street, the physiotherapist at Arsenal whose duties extended to the England team. Fred had borrowed a portable tape recorder and taken it with him to England's training base where they were preparing for their friendly international game against the Republic of Ireland. Even better than just asking the players to record a message, Fred had asked England Captain Kevin Keegan to interview them while they were on the coach. 'Honorary Radio Marsden member Kevin' set the scene, explaining how the team had just left their hotel and were now on their way to play the match at Wembley Stadium and how he was going to move around the coach recording players' thoughts and some get-well messages from them. Kevin was a very polished and professional reporter and interviewed star players such as goalkeeper Ray Clements as well as Stuart Pearson, the eventual scorer of the goal in their 1–1 draw, Gordon Hill, Colin Todd and West Ham's Trevor Brooking. I cannot imagine the current England captain agreeing to such a task and it just proved what a good person Kevin Keegan was, not just as a footballer but also as an accomplished radio interviewer.

BOB CHAMPION – Professional jump jockey

Bob Champion became a celebrity due to his real-life story. In 1979, with his riding career at its peak, it all came crashing down when he contracted testicular cancer. Thankfully, he was successfully treated for it at The Royal Marsden Hospital and made a full recovery. Just seven months after his treatment, Bob returned to professional riding, having worked incredibly hard to get himself back in the saddle. He then stunned the racing world by riding Aldaniti to victory in the 1981 Grand National. This event is known as the most punishing jump race in the world, regularly taking the lives of horses and seriously injuring jockeys, so everyone in The Royal Marsden watched the race that Saturday afternoon with their hands over their eyes, fearing Bob would take a fall. By the finish, there wasn't a dry eye in the hospital as he guided Aldaniti into the winner's enclosure at Aintree. There was an outpouring of emotion throughout the country that weekend, such was the respect the nation had for his courage and tenacity in overcoming his illness in such a memorable way. Bob embarked on a massive fundraising venture for The Royal Marsden Hospital, in appreciation of his successful treatment. His story went on to be covered in the 1984 film

Champions, starring John Hurt.

Bob even helped Radio Marsden. One of our volunteers was recording an interview with a patient and the lady talked of her own love of horses and her ambition to meet her hero, none other than Bob Champion. When I heard this, I thought I should try and see if Radio Marsden could make that ambition come true, given Bob's connection with the hospital. I thought about how I could go about making contact with him and decided to phone *Sporting Life*, the newspaper known for its specialist coverage of horse racing. I was put through to their news desk and explained who I was and if by any chance, they could help our patient. I was hopeful, but not prepared for what happened next. 'No problem,' said the person I was speaking to, 'I'll give you Bob's phone number.' A few minutes later, having thanked him profusely, I sat at my desk summoning up the courage to make a call to someone I had never met but was, at that time, a massive celebrity and an icon of his sport. I called the number and the phone rang a couple of times until a voice answered, 'Bob Champion.' I introduced myself and apologised for disturbing him before explaining my request. Bob was the same nice person on the phone as the media portrayed him. He immediately agreed to help and explained how he was due at The Royal Marsden in a few days' time for a check-up and would drop by the ward and find our 'horse-mad' patient. The Radio Marsden volunteer returned to that patient's bedside the following week and she told him how excited she was to meet Bob Champion, who had indeed dropped in to see her. Our volunteer said she looked and sounded a lot more perky compared with when he had first met her and reckoned that was down to Bob's visit having such a beneficial effect on her health. Just how difficult would that be to arrange these days when most sporting celebrities are surrounded by agents and PR people? Sadly, gone are the times when a phone call to a newspaper could result in their news desk passing on the direct number of a sporting icon such as Bob Champion.

CHAPTER 8

Living dangerously

My life was busy enough, trying to balance family and work, but I still tried to arrange time between to go out and record interviews whenever we received a positive response to a letter. One day in 1987, I took a call from the hospital asking if I would like to spend a day attending a fundraising venture. I was worried this might involve sitting on a committee or rattling a charity tin on a windy street corner somewhere. However, it turned out to be something far more exciting, which at one stage also became seriously dangerous. The fundraising event in question was a day out on the River Thames with some celebrities and somehow involved a double decker London bus. It sounded intriguing and I agreed to attend, setting off early one morning armed with my trusty tape recorder and a camera. If I had known what was ahead, I would also have carried a life jacket, for reasons that soon will become obvious.

David Kirke was a member of Oxford University's *Dangerous Sports Club* and had made a name for himself back in 1979 by making the first ever 'bungy' – later renamed 'bungee' – jump and inventing the sport in the process. David's first leap was made when he launched himself off Bristol's Clifton Suspension Bridge and down into the Avon

Gorge with just a couple of elasticated cords tied to his feet to break his fall before he hit the water.

David had suggested organising a 'never done before' publicity stunt to aid The Royal Marsden Hospital's 'One Day for Life' cancer appeal. His idea? To drive the London double decker bus under Tower Bridge, a feat that certainly had 'never been done before'. There was a tenuous link to an event that occurred in 1952 when a London bus had jumped over Tower Bridge but that had not been a stunt. Ten people were injured after the number 78 bus, driven by Albert Gunter, approached the centre of the bridge, only for him to see the road ahead drop away as the bridge's two spans started to rise accidentally. Quick-thinking Albert floored the accelerator and managed to jump the gap that had opened up in front of him. He made it safely to the other side and for his brave efforts, the bus company rewarded him a £10 bonus, worth about £300 these days.

David's plan was to fill a London bus with a variety of celebrities willing to ride on it for charity. The most well-known participants were Major Ronald Ferguson, father of the then Sarah, Duchess of York. The Hon. Angus Ogilvy, the husband of Princess Alexandra of Kent, and Graham Chapman, one of the stars of the Monty Python team. The news media would be there to witness the feat which included by special invitation, Radio Marsden. Clearly the event appeared to be an act of sheer madness, but I could not refuse the opportunity to see for myself. I would be the eyes and ears of our patients by recording a commentary, and with a bit of luck, having an opportunity to record interviews with some of the celebrities.

I arrived at Tower Pier at the designated time, along with

what seemed to be the entire world's press corps. We were all herded aboard a large river boat, the type usually used to carry tourists up and down the Thames. It duly set off and sailed out into the section of the river between London and Tower Bridge known as the Pool of London. Our river boat slowed as it approached the middle of the Thames and turned to face downstream. I looked at Tower Bridge and suddenly saw a tug emerging from under its spans towing a giant pontoon, on which was firmly strapped a London double decker bus with all the celebrities aboard it, waving enthusiastically. Tethered behind the bus were two giant inflatable animals, an elephant and a kangaroo, billowing in the air. I later discovered they were named Nellie and Hopalong. 'Rule Britannia' blared out from the bus over a hastily rigged tannoy system. The tug hauling the pontoon steamed slowly under Tower Bridge, successfully fulfilling the promise made by the *Dangerous Sports Club's* David Kirke. In the distance I could just make out a figure in the driver's cab, so, you could say, this was indeed the first and probably last London bus to be 'driven' under Tower Bridge.

The sight of all this going on, while certainly mesmerising to watch, was of no great interest to Radio Marsden's audience who depended on sound for their entertainment. I had my tape recorder with me but other than my fairly banal commentary on what I was seeing, backed by the tinny sound of 'Rule Britannia', I had little to record. As the bus continued its journey under the bridge and headed closer towards the press boat, another person with a tape recorder approached me. He turned out to be a reporter from LBC Radio who told me the plan was for the tug to tow the pontoon with its bus to Tower Pier where it would dock along with our river boat and then all the press would swarm aboard it to photograph and interview the celebrities. He said that would be a complete scrum and he reckoned the only way for the two of us 'radio reporters' – really meaning him the professional and me, the mere amateur from Radio Marsden – to record some interviews would be to get onboard the bus before it docked at the pier. Just to make polite conversation, I agreed, and then he said he would go and talk to whoever was in charge on the bridge of our riverboat and see what could be arranged. Before I could think of anything else and not being exactly sure what I was letting myself into, I mumbled what a great idea that was. He soon returned with the 'good' news that he had convinced our captain to steer his riverboat parallel to the tug's pontoon and to match its speed, getting as close as possible to give us a few seconds to make the leap on to it. Now we were talking here about jumping from a moving riverboat onto a moving pontoon, in the middle of the Pool of London, 'One small step for man' across one of the fastest moving tidal rivers in the country. Few who had fallen into this part of the Thames had ever survived and I was about to risk exactly that without a life jacket. Fortunately, there was no time to consider how reckless his plan was as the boat suddenly turned 90 degrees and travelled parallel to the pontoon. A deckhand slid back a railing, Mr LBC jumped first and I followed. We both just managed to scramble onto the pontoon before the riverboat pulled away. Once I recovered from the recklessness of this exercise, it soon became apparent my new 'best radio friend' had been right. We were the only two reporters aboard the bus and had the celebrities to ourselves until it docked at Tower Pier.

Having cleared my head of all thoughts of how my leap of faith could have gone badly wrong, I boarded the bus. The first 'celebrity' I met was the Hon. Angus Ogilvy, a very personable and easy-to-talk to man who was very much the modern husband to Princess Alexandra. On his marriage to the Princess, he had refused the Queen's offer of both an earldom and a grace-and favour apartment in a royal palace. He explained that he was on the bus in his role of president of the Imperial Cancer Research Fund, at the time the largest research fund in Europe. We finished the interview with a get-well message for the patients before I headed down the bus to the next celebrity whose voice was even more aristocratic that that of the Hon Ogilvy, but there the similarities definitely ended. Arabella Fifi was scantily dressed in just a bikini and admitted it had been a freezing cold and rather wet journey for her down the Thames that morning. I failed to discover exactly what she did or how she fitted the celebrity profile of the rest of the passengers so could only surmise it was that bikini and the posh voice. She did manage to record a get-well message for the patients with me averting my gaze.

Moving upstairs in the bus, I met Graham Chapman, a star of *Monty Python's Flying Circus* and films such as *Life of Brian*, in which he had the leading role, and *The Meaning of Life*. This was 1987 and Graham told me he was not happy at the moment with his Python colleagues. I asked if he had met up with them recently and he said he definitely had not. It turned out he was not talking to them very much at all. I think he had let the cork out of the bottle as he became very animated and told me how he had 'really really' fallen out with them but might be friendly again sometime in the future depending on how they behaved. I tried to coax a little more information out of him about what had happened to cause such a serious bust-up with his fellow performers. I adopted my best persuasive charm and played the sympathy card. Asking if he could tell 'all the patients in The Royal Marsden Hospital' a little bit more about it. After all, I had the feeling I was about to uncover our first scoop! Sadly, he immediately stopped himself and admitted he had very nearly said too much and that he had better keep quiet about it all and say no more on the subject. Sadly, any chance of a Radio Marsden scoop went out the window. His get-well message to our patients was very bizarre and I later decided not to broadcast it. Maybe I was being oversensitive given the nature of the illness that brings patients into the Marsden, but I thought his rather abrupt instruction 'Why don't you get well? Really, lying around there all day long. Just get up and get better quickly and do us all a favour,' wouldn't go down so well with our listeners on the wards, whether or not they were fans of this famous *Monty Python* star. I loved Graham Chapman and the rest of the Python team but, similar to the decision I made in not playing Spike Milligan's rant about cigarettes, I just couldn't see any benefit in broadcasting this message. I am sure our patients would be very happy to be able to think themselves better if they could, with or without the need of a prompt from Graham Chapman, despite the fact he had qualified as a medical doctor before deciding on a career in comedy.

My next interview subject was the very glamorous Kathy Lloyd, one of *The Sun* newspaper's early Page Three girls and, at the time, 'Face of 1987' for the *Daily Star*. That newspaper had asked her to join the bus that day. She told me her job as 'the face' involved attending dinners and events such as this one. Her get-well message ended with a loud and suggestive kiss into the microphone, which I liked a lot and, when we later played it on air, it certainly cheered up all our male patients.

The bus driver's cab was occupied by Major Ronald Ferguson who climbed down out of it and agreed to talk to me. He was very jovial and gave a detailed report of the bus's journey that morning. He told me the driving conditions along the Thames had been smooth, but a little overcast with some drizzle. He then added that no mines had been spotted! Major Ferguson had recently hosted a cancer research polo event at Ham attended by Royal Marsden legend Bob Champion, our Grand National- winning jockey, along with HRH The Prince of Wales. Sadly, this had not been an event to which Radio Marsden had been invited, it seemed we were only given the dangerous events such as this one on the Thames, rather than risking our attendance at anything too posh.

The Dangerous Sports Club member, David Kirke, explained to me how they had actually put the bus on the pontoon further downriver with the help of a large crane. His other more bizarre future plans included rolling a large bubble towards France and a flying horse called Pegasus. Whether any of these events ever came to fruition, remains unknown. After about an hour, the bus on its pontoon with its cargo of celebrity passengers and the two intrepid radio reporters, finally berthed at Tower Pier. Just as the LBC reporter had predicted, all the members of the press rushed aboard but I just managed to snatch a few minutes with TV presenter Selina Scott who had been waiting at the pier for the bus to arrive. Selina was a celebrity in her own right having co-presented the BBC's first *Breakfast Time* show along with Frank Bough. She told me she was actually there today in a working capacity, covering the event for the American CBS network. I cheekily told Selina our interview would be 'between one news gatherer and another' but this rather unprofessional attempt at equalisation did not make much of an impression on her. Selina was very honest and told me her life as a TV presenter was certainly not all glamour and luxury. Earlier in the day, her film crew had failed to meet her as arranged at the bus's departure point. She had no choice but to jump on a riverboat heading up the Thames which got her to Tower Pier just in time to rendezvous with them to do a planned TV interview with Major Ferguson. Selina was a class act and provided the day's best get-well message for our patients.

Finally, it was time for the bus to make its return journey down the Thames back to Cherry Tree Pier where it had started out earlier in the day. Off it 'drove', still firmly attached on its pontoon, but now with just one lonely celebrity passenger onboard. This was a rather forlorn-looking Graham Chapman who only had his pipe for company. He had asked to stay on the bus for the return trip as he had left his car back at the starting point, with little thought as to how he would get back to recover it.

The double decker bus minutes after it had been 'driven' under London's Tower Bridge.

Month Python actor, Graham Chapman, on the bus for its return journey to Cherry Tree Pier to retrieve his car!

CHAPTER 9

It can be a serious business

Going out and meeting celebrities for an interview was always a very interesting part of running Radio Marsden, with the added excitement when they sometimes came along to our studio in the hospital. However, there were times when the seriousness of patients' illnesses, particularly when they involved young people, would be brought home to me and gave rise to an opportunity to prove the real worth of our hospital radio. In most cases this could be the sight of a patient breaking into a wide smile on hearing their favourite record or being able to thank a member of the hospital's team by nominating them to receive our weekly Staff Award. However, nothing prepared me for a benefit of hospital radio I had never considered but would stay with me for ever. One Friday morning I received a call from a nurse working on the Princess Chula Children's Ward. She told me about a young patient who was sadly entering the last days of her life. Her mother had mentioned to the nurse that, while she had many photographs to remember her by, what she would miss most of all was the sound of her voice. The nurse had thought about this and contacted me to see if Radio Marsden could do an interview with the young girl and give her mother a copy of the recording for her to keep as a lasting memory of her daughter.

This was the most moving and unexpected request I had ever received and, before I could give thought to the responsibility that went with it, I immediately agreed. Arriving at the hospital later that day, I was still uncertain as to the best way to approach the task, given the sad circumstances. Just what do you talk to a child about when you know they may only have a few days to live? I decided the only way was to put the circumstances out of my mind and do it exactly the same as if it was any other young patient. When I met the mother, I asked if she would prefer to just have a chat with her daughter which I would record, but she said she would find that far too emotional and would be too tearful, so would prefer to leave it to me to talk to her. The girl was about 9 years old and I asked her all the things I hoped someone her age might want to talk about. She told me how she spent her time on the ward, what her favourite food was, the pop groups she liked the best, all about her family, her pets and a lot more. She was so easy to talk to and the time flew by as we chatted. After about twenty minutes, she suddenly started to get very tired, so I rounded-up the interview and said my goodbyes.

I went down to the Radio Marsden studio to prepare a copy of the cassette to give to her mother. As I sat at the mixing desk with the tapes in the machines ready to do the copying, I suddenly thought that this particular interview was not one to be heard by any ears other than those of her mother and her family. Removing the original tape, I broke off the two plastic lugs on the back of the cassette, to make sure it could never be recorded over, I wrote the girl's name on the label and headed back up to Princess Chula Ward where I handed it to her mother. I left the hospital that day suitably humbled and thinking of the devastating effect cancer can have on such a young life and her family.

This had been an important job for Radio Marsden, and I was proud to have been able to respond to the nurse and provide the mother with a recording of her daughter's voice which she would now have for ever. After the weekend, that same nurse called me again, this time to let me know the little girl had died over the weekend. She said how grateful the girl's mother was for that recording and how it would be played forever as a reminder of her brave and beautiful daughter. This only happened once during my time at Radio Marsden, but every new volunteer was always told of the event, just in case it should occur again when they might be similarly called upon to record what had been for me, and I'm sure would be for them, the hardest interview they would ever have to do.

CHAPTER 10

Programme development

Abiding by its mantra of 'quality over quantity', Radio Marsden took time before increasing its programme schedule to ensure we only broadcast ones which would be of real interest to our patients. This policy was based upon the fact we were in a cancer hospital and our patients suffered more ups and downs; feeling under the weather one day and then better the next, due to the effects of the chemotherapy and many other treatments administered to fight their particular illness.

As time went on, we realised we didn't have to be totally dependent on just record requests and competitions to entertain the patients, as there were other programme opportunities which could be equally of interest to them. Some of the new programmes were run by volunteers with expert knowledge on a subject, as was the case with our classical music hour *A Touch of Class* which was started by the secretary of the Carshalton Gramophone Society who offered to present a weekly programme of music. He was soon joined by his great friend from a rival organisation, the Banstead Recorded Music Society and for many years the two of them entertained the patients with their weekly programme, which was always interesting as they demonstrated their deep knowledge and understanding of classical music as they talked between playing that evening's chosen pieces.

Some of the volunteers formed a drama workshop and would meet in the studio at weekends to write and record their own documentaries and comedy shows. One production is permanently etched on my memory, the comedy action-drama series featuring a character called Rick Razor as a spoof James Bond. That was guaranteed to give patients a good laugh whenever a new episode hit the airwaves.

We had always made sure Radio Marsden reached out to the children in the hospital. Sutton had its Princess Chula Ward which treated both very young children and teenagers. In addition to including them in our normal programmes, we also produced a weekly cassette tape which featured again all the music they had asked for in that week's request programme and including additional, age-related items. The ward employed a full-time play therapist who could then play the tape to either an individual patient or a group. We also helped with the annual Princess Chula Ward Christmas party by organising the disco and having a team of Radio Marsden helpers there on the day. One of the highlights of the party was often a visit by some of the officers and sailors from the navy destroyer, HMS *Antrim*. This ship had adopted the ward a few years earlier and, whenever it was in port, members of the crew, impressively dressed in their best uniforms, would visit the hospital, ladened with presents for the children.

One programme I was keen to put on air was *Marsden People* which featured a member of the hospital staff who we would interview between playing some of their favourite music. This was particularly beneficial to the patients when it featured a doctor or a consultant who would talk about their work and often their life or hobbies away from the Marsden. This programme was well received by the patients and I recall one telling me how she liked hearing about a particular doctor who had featured on that week's programme, as it would give her something other than how she was feeling to talk about when she next saw him. The only problem with this programme was the time it took to arrange and this could stretch to months. Once they did agree, they were not always available to come into the studio for a live programme, so I had to make a daytime visit to the hospital to record their interview and then add their music choice later. I recall one high-level consultant requesting an initial meeting for me to explain the format of the programme and to discuss my questions before a follow-up visit could be arranged to record the actual interview. Sadly, I was unable to do as many of these as I would have liked due to work commitments, but I would recommend it to other hospital radio stations as an excellent way of breaking down the wall of initial nervousness that can often exist between a patient and their doctors.

Here are a few details of just some of the many programmes we were broadcasting:

MONDAY-GO-ROUND/THE WEEK AHEAD

A magazine-type programme featuring patient interviews, a news quiz, celebrity birthdays, a welcome to all our new patients, book prizes, hospital services information interspersed with light music.

SHOWCASE

A special presentation each week, including productions from the drama workshop, interviews with hospital staff and featuring well-known pieces of classical music.

NIGHTCAP

A medley of soothing music and poetry. Each evening's broadcast finished with this programme. This nightly one-hour programme was designed to round-off a patient's day by offering them an hour of light music to help them relax and, hopefully, drop off to sleep.

MARSDEN PEOPLE

A chance for patients to hear members of the hospital staff talking about their life and work and playing their favourite records.

CLASSICAL CORNER/A TOUCH OF CLASS

All types of classical music presented by our two experts from local music societies.

TAKE IT EASY

The main competition of the week with prizes galore, patients' own jokes and a selection of light music seasoned with humour and snippets of useless information.

MARSDEN MAGAZINE

Interviews with stars and personalities, quiz features, documentaries, comedy and music.

ONCE UPON A CHULA

Stories, poems, jokes and music aimed at the youngsters in the children's ward.

There is always a risk of attracting 'wannabe DJs' to hospital radio. People who may seem creditable initially but are actually more interested in trying to evolve into god's gift to Radio 1 rather than being part of a team dedicated to the patients. Fortunately, Radio Marsden attracted very few of these as many of our new volunteers first came into the studio before or after visiting a patient they knew in the hospital. Our interview procedure was also designed to spot anyone who might be looking to use us as a training ground for possible professional radio work, rather than genuinely wanting to give their time to help out and entertain our patients. To ensure our broadcasts maintained as high a standard as possible, and to maintain our policy of being 100 per cent entertaining to our patients, once a month I would arrange a 'programme monitoring week'. A set of two-hour C120 cassettes would be provided for each evening and presenters would make a recording of their programme as it went out. I would then collect the tapes at the end of the week and take them home to listen to. In fact, most of the monitoring of those tapes took place 'on the road' as I was often making long drives to visit customers. I would play an evening's programme recordings and make notes on a small dictation machine. I would then use that to write a short report for each evening's team, not just mentioning my negative comments but, more importantly for good morale, highlighting all the positives. These were, after all, volunteers not highly paid members of a radio station. I felt it important to concentrate on the good aspects of their programmes and lightly touch on any area needing improvement. This seemed to work well, and I don't recall anyone flouncing out following a negative monitoring report and any shortcomings were usually corrected when it came to the next month's tapes.

My sons Ben and Sam take a turn in running the disco at a Princess Chula Ward party

Young patients and volunteers enjoy the entertainment at a Princess Chula Ward party, with some of the crew from HMS Antrim *seen in the background.*

WHAT'S ON RadioMarsden on channel two

mondays

7.00 - 8.00 pm — **GOOD VIBRATIONS**

Top Twenty records past and present, introduced by Graham Banks.

8.00 - 9.00 — **ALBUM TRACKING**

the best in pop music on L.P., played by Roger Bonner.

tuesdays

7.00 - 9.00 pm — **RECORD REQUEST SHOW**

David Peschier and Andrew Robertson present your choice in music, plus messages from your friends and relatives, and a weekly award to a nominated member of the hospital staff.

wednesdays

7.00 - 8.00 pm — **THE LIGHT PROGRAMME**

Martin Ashton and Paul Preston introduce a selection of light music. Phil Boys presents the weekly competition, and interviews the prize winners.

8.00 - 9.00 — **A TOUCH OF CLASS**

classical music and informative commentary from members of the Carshalton Gramophone Society.

thursday

7.00 - 8.00 pm — **MARSDEN MAGAZINE**

news reports and voices from around the Royal Marsden, including 'Patient of the Week'. And there are star interviews, film and theatre reviews, talks, poetry, and much more. James Pringle and Bob Pix are in the studio, and Keith Newman, Maureen George and Trish Kinane are out and about with roving microphones.

An early programme guide circa. 1972.

Get to know...

Radio Marsden

Your Bedside Companion!

Monday at 7pm

The Week Ahead

A look at the coming week on Radio Marsden, together with music, interviews and special features.

Tuesday at 7pm

The Record Request Show

Two hours of music that you have requested, or has been requested for you by your friends and relatives. Featuring the STAFF AWARD and POP THE CORK presentations.

Wednesday at 7pm

Take It Easy

Ninety minutes of light music seasoned with humour and snippets of information. Featuring the weekly LUCK OF THE DRAW competition.

Wednesday at 8.30pm

A Touch of Class

An hour of classical music with informative commentary.

Thursday at 7pm

Marsden Magazine

Interviews with stars and personalities, talks, debates, drama, documentaries, music, comedy, panel games and special presentations.

RADIO MARSDEN IS ON CHANNEL 2

A few years later, our programme guide had become a little more sophisticated – well the typefaces had!

The Touch of Class *team. (Left) Bill Wilson and (right) Andy Simpson entertain patients with their knowledge and choice of classical music.*

CHAPTER 11

Royalty

The Royal Marsden Hospital in Sutton has been fortunate over the years in welcoming more than its fair share of royal visitors. These began with HM Queen Elizabeth II travelling to Sutton in 1963 to officially open the new hospital. That was six years before Radio Marsden started, so it was not until 1973 that we had our first chance of being involved with the next royal visit. This time it was HM Queen Elizabeth the Queen Mother who came in July to open the new Bud Flanagan Ward, a special sterile unit for the treatment of patients suffering from various forms of leukaemia. I was told royal protocol meant Radio Marsden would not be allowed to interview Her Majesty, nor would her schedule allow time for her to visit our studio. We still decided we should try and be involved by presenting a special daytime programme with, as best we could, commentaries covering her progress around the various parts of the hospital and maybe getting the thoughts from some of the patients she had met.

The problems of putting on such a programme were clear when the team met to discuss the event. In addition to abiding by the strict protocol surrounding such events, there would also be a high level of security in the hospital that day, resulting in us being excluded from many of the locations the

Queen Mother would be visiting. We had to be content with placing our volunteers as close as possible to areas where Her Majesty would be, and then having them rush back to the studio to report to our listening audience what they had seen and heard. It was also decided our coverage should start with me doing an outside broadcast commentary describing the scene, from the time Her Majesty's car first entered the approach road to the hospital. I carried out some reconnaissance and decided the flat roof above the children's ward would be the best vantage point to survey the scene as it unfolded below me. The hospital gave their permission for Radio Marsden to do the programme and allowed me to access my outside viewing area.

The event would, as usual, involve me climbing out of windows, this time to gain access to the roof where I perched myself, somewhat precariously, as I looked across to the long drive leading from Downs Road to the hospital's main entrance. Andrew Robertson, our programme controller, had a contact who was willing to lend us a rather valuable Shure wireless microphone. This would enable me to do my outside commentary without us having to run cables half the length of the hospital, which would not have been permitted on the day of a royal visit. Having the use of what was then regarded as 'high-tech kit' was great, as the microphone would transmit my voice back to the studio where its receiver would be, so no wires or cables were necessary. The only drawback to this, apart from not having any previous experience of using a radio microphone, was that, while I could transmit my commentary, I would be unable to hear anything coming to me from the studio. We came up with the idea of having someone from the studio programme team monitoring me 'off air' through the Pre-Fade Listening facility which was now a welcome feature on our new mixer. I would give them a countdown on that mixer channel starting from *5* and they would put me on air a couple of seconds after I said *1* which sounded a good solution. The equipment came packed in its own specially designed briefcase containing, not just the microphone, but also its bulky transmitter. These were early times for this type of wireless microphone technology, which is now commonplace throughout the broadcasting industry. Pardon the pun but, at the time, we were very 'un-Shure' as to whether it would work, and our concerns were not misplaced.

On the day, I climbed through the window to get to reach my commentary position early and looked down on the scene below. The hospital's drive was lined with excited schoolchildren enthusiastically waving their Union Jack flags, while trying to peer between the line of police officers stationed along the car's intended route, to see what was happening. I turned on the radio microphone and gave the agreed countdown before launching into my commentary. I set the scene for the Radio Marsden listeners as best I could and it wasn't long before loud cheers could be heard as, flanked by motorcycle outriders, Her Majesty's stately Rolls Royce came into view and glided down the drive towards the hospital. I edged along the flat roof to the corner of the building to gain a better view of the entrance below me. It really was a splendid sight, and I did my best to emulate the great broadcaster Sir Richard Dimbleby, by changing the tone of my voice to bring a little more gravitas to the proceeding. The car finally drew up at the entrance and out stepped the Queen Mother to be greeted by the chairman of The Royal Marsden board and various civic dignitaries.

They then accompanied her into the hospital which took Her Majesty out of my sight, but I continued commenting, giving the names of those she would be meeting in the long line-up of hospital staff patiently waiting to be introduced. This was thanks to having been given a full copy of the day's briefing notes which meticulously listed every detail of the visit, including all those being introduced. Finally, I signed off my commentary by saying, 'and with the Queen Mother having entered the hospital to start this historic visit, this is David returning you to the Radio Marsden studio.'

I made my precarious journey back along the roof and climbed in through the window before making my way back to the studio. I felt rather pleased with myself, and maybe a little smug, thinking it had all gone rather well for my first time doing an outside commentary, and dared to hope the rest of the programme team would think the same. On entering our room, there was no round of applause, almost the opposite, as I was met with a sea of glum faces. Had it not been as good as I thought? Or were they all feeling a bit sheepish to be in the company of Radio Marsden's own version of Richard Dimbleby? Sadly, I soon heard the reason for the lack of celebration. It turned out the long distance between the microphone's transmitter and its receiver back in the studio, combined with the hospital's heavily lined walls, necessary to contain the radioactive radiation equipment, had conspired to make my 'Dimbleby moment' almost non-existent. They had clearly heard the first ten minutes of my commentary as I had set the scene, but as soon as I moved across to the far corner of the roof for a better view of the drive – not something I had rehearsed during the previous day's short test – the signal from the wireless microphone dropped out and could not be picked up by its receiver in the studio. This left the studio presenters with no option but to ad lib in the hope I would be heard from again, which sadly didn't happen. They covered the time that should have been the rest of my commentary by playing music until another team member came in to report that Her Majesty had arrived on one of the wards. To say I was disappointed was an understatement and I continue to joke to this day that it really was my 'finest hour' as a commentator, that's if anyone apart from myself could have actually heard it! The rest of the team did a great job with the remainder of our royal visit programme, which was well received by the patients. They all heard it was a special day for the hospital and the Queen Mother was a hugely popular royal figure. A few days later I was pleased to receive a letter from the hospital administrator, thanking Radio Marsden for doing such a splendid job in covering the visit 'so enthusiastically'. I didn't dare to think he knew of my disaster with the scene-setting commentary and I never trusted a wireless microphone again.

Just over ten years later, in 1984, I was called into the administrator's office to be briefed about our next royal visitor. This time it was to be the most popular member of the royal family at that time, HRH Diana Princess of Wales would be coming to the hospital on 21st February to open another new leukaemia unit. However, I was told this time the security levels would be even higher than they had been for the Queen Mother's visit. I was firmly instructed that Radio Marsden volunteers would not be allowed in the hospital that day and no special programme coverage was possible. All doors opening onto any of the corridors on the Princess's route through the hospital would be locked in advance and remain so throughout the duration of her visit. That would include our studio which was on the main corridor the Princess would be walking through shortly after her arrival. This was very sad news for Radio Marsden and the patients, as our previous royal visit programme over a decade earlier had been well received and gave everyone a chance to enjoy the day, whether or not they saw the royal visitor on their ward. I argued my case with the fairly new administrator but was told it was all about the security measures imposed on them and was not a criticism of Radio Marsden. I had to settle for that and briefed our programme leaders accordingly. On the day, the turnout was even bigger than it had been for the Queen Mother, as the Princess's arrival was greeted by even more local school children lining that same drive I had previously, rather unsuccessfully, commented on. It was a pity there would be no second chance for Radio Marsden to cover this one as we had learnt a lot in the last ten years and now had far better equipment, including being able to solve the previous problem with the wireless microphone. I was sure we could have broadcast a far more polished and professional programme to the patients marking the Princess's visit, but it was not to be.

On the day, the royal visit proceeded without any Radio Marsden involvement so imagine my frustration when, shortly after Princess Diana had left the hospital, I received a call from one of our members. He told me how excited his mother, also a Radio Marsden volunteer, had been on meeting Princess Diana earlier in the day! I told him that could not have happened, but he went on to explain how she and another team member had gone to the hospital earlier that morning, seemingly ignorant of the fact none of us were allowed to be there due to the intense security lockdown ahead of the arrival of Her Royal Highness. They had parked and entered the hospital as usual, signed for the Radio Marsden room key and gone in to select the music for their evening programme. They had left the studio door open, and an hour or so later, were shocked when in walked an unexpected visitor, none other than Princess Diana! They said her eyes lit up as she said 'Now this looks interesting' as the most famous woman in the world spotted our studio mixing desk. The two Radio Marsden volunteers, having managed to recover their composure after their initial shock, explained that this was the Radio Marsden studio. The Princess immediately followed up with, 'How exciting, are you broadcasting now?' They explained they were not on air just then but stopped short of saying we had been banned because of her visit! Princess Diana looked a little disappointed but said how good it had been to meet them both. Suddenly, in rushed an embarrassed hospital administrator who quickly ushered the Princess out of our studio. Seems she had been walking past our open door and decided to drop in. Her host had continued on a good few yards before suddenly realising his royal VIP guest was no longer at his side, forcing him to retrace his steps to find where she had suddenly disappeared to.

I was devastated, what a missed opportunity. If only management had taken a more reasonable approach. We were, after all, highly trusted within the hospital with access granted to almost all areas. However, it was the time when many IRA terrorist attacks were taking lives. They had already started again in 1973, the time of the Queen Mother's visit, but by 1984 they had risen dramatically. Since the Harrods bombing the previous December, there had been a heightened security presence, especially around the royal family. Given that background, I understood the hospital's concerns which were heavily influenced by the police and other security forces. The fact some of our volunteers had just walked into out studio unchallenged on the morning of the royal visit made a bit of a mockery of the reasons I had been given as to why we could not do another special programme. I thought we should have been allowed to be involved, just as we had for the previous royal visit and it was a missed opportunity for Radio Marsden. I could only imagine how we all would have felt had we been allowed to put out a programme that day and Princess Diana dropped into the studio to, just maybe, give a cheery 'Hello' to all the patients. That would have been amazing.

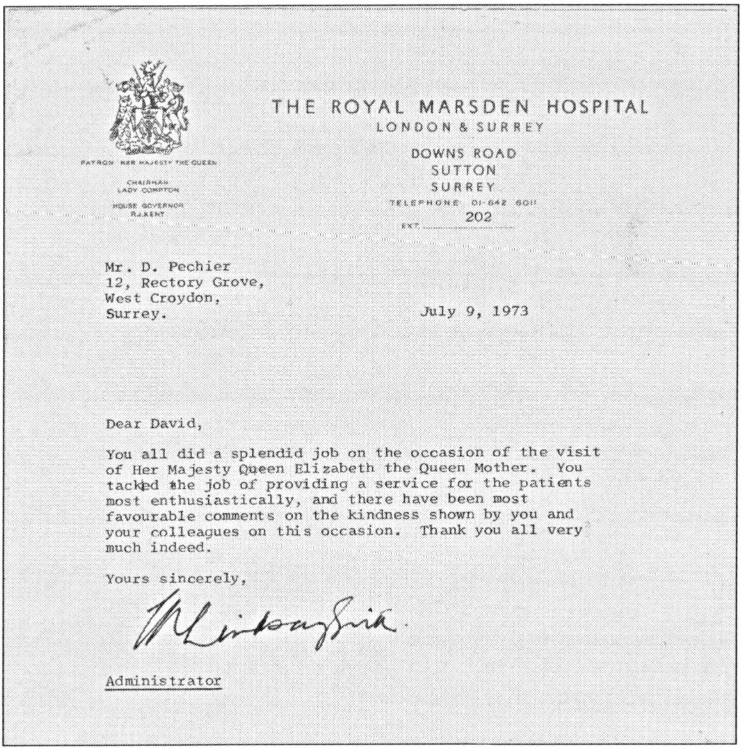

PATRON HER MAJESTY THE QUEEN

CHAIRMAN
LADY COMPTON

HOUSE GOVERNOR
R.J.KENT

THE ROYAL MARSDEN HOSPITAL
LONDON & SURREY

DOWNS ROAD
SUTTON
SURREY

TELEPHONE 01-642 6011
EXT. 202

Mr. D. Pechier
12, Rectory Grove,
West Croydon,
Surrey.

July 9, 1973

Dear David,

You all did a splendid job on the occasion of the visit of Her Majesty Queen Elizabeth the Queen Mother. You tackled the job of providing a service for the patients most enthusiastically, and there have been most favourable comments on the kindness shown by you and your colleagues on this occasion. Thank you all very much indeed.

Yours sincerely,

Administrator

It was always good to receive a complimentary letter from the boss!

CHAPTER 12

Full circle – we broadcast to Fulham Road

It was 1980 and everything at Radio Marsden was running smoothly and we had sufficient volunteers to form teams of people to enable us to present programmes every evening from Monday to Thursday. The Occupational Therapy Department in The Royal Marsden Hospital in Fulham Road had long stopped their weekly programme of playing music and their collection of records had been transferred to Sutton when Radio Marsden was first set up. During one of our regular Radio Marsden meetings, a member suggested maybe it was time to consider also broadcasting programmes to The Royal Marsden in Fulham Road. It seemed a crazy idea but everyone round the table showed great enthusiasm at the thought of almost doubling our listeners. We all agreed that if we extended our coverage to Fulham Road, it was vital we also continued to preserve the same close relationship with the patients we had always maintained in Sutton. This relationship was sustained by all our volunteers making frequent visits to the wards and by having special features such as our weekly Staff Award. We would need to do the same at Fulham Road, with them having their own programme teams for each evening, just as we had in Sutton.

It would be impractical to find new recruits ourselves,

or to ask some of our volunteers from Sutton to travel to Fulham Road each week to host a programme, as nearly all lived locally to our hospital and arrived straight from work to present their evening programmes. It was clear we would need separate teams going into the Fulham Road hospital to do the ward visits and take part in our programmes. To make it work we would also need a music-quality landline to carry the Radio Marsden output to Fulham Road. This would be linked into their hospital's radio equipment so the patients could hear our programmes through their bedside headphones. I was stunned by the estimate of £440 a year to rent the landline and, even with us registered as a charity, there was no discount from the Post Office, the forerunner of British Telecom. Thankfully, we had sufficient in the bank from our own fundraising efforts to cover the landline cost but hoped we might also receive some financial help from Fulham Road's Junior League of Friends who were to be our main point of contact in our discussions to see if the project was workable.

It is important to understand that the hospital in Sutton where Radio Marsden is based, is in fact the 'Surrey branch' of The Royal Marsden and those words are carved in the stone alongside its name at the entrance to the driveway to the hospital. The original Royal Marsden was founded and remains in operation to this day in London's Fulham Road and I was always made aware of that being the parent hospital from my very first day. It was the same when we came to negotiate the best way for Radio Marsden to be heard by the patients in their imposing old building in Chelsea, which even has a grand piano in its entrance hall. This is played regularly by volunteers and certainly fulfils its role of relaxing both old and new patients as it is often the first thing they see, and sometimes hear, as they walk in through the doors of the hospital. In 1980, Fulham Road had not one, but two, League of Friends organisations. Its namesake for those of a mature age, and the Junior League, an enthusiastic group of younger people, who mainly joined to become involved in fundraising for the hospital. To say they were all rather posh would be an understatement, in fact they were ultra-posh while still being nice and friendly. My first meeting in the Fulham Road hospital was a world away from those Radio Marsden ones held in Sutton. Such was the grandeur of their conference room, I felt as if I was attending a job interview in a merchant bank in the City, rather than sitting in a pioneering cancer hospital. Myself and a couple of others from Sutton sat quietly through the first part of the meeting. One item on the Junior League's agenda was an update on the progress of their Royal Marsden Ball, an event I had never heard of before, let alone attended, but then I was based at Sutton, the lowly 'Surrey branch'! This Ball was held annually, and that year would be at Park Lane's *Grosvenor House Hotel.* Organised and hosted by the Junior League of Friends, its aim was to raise at least £30,000 for the hospital. I listened in awe as they discussed the arrangements for that year's event. When it came to discussing the raffle prizes, one committee member excitedly announced she had a contact at a travel agents who had offered to donate a pair of airline tickets to any European destination. That was impressive and suitable murmurs of appreciation were heard from around the table. Hardly had the ripples of gratitude subsided when up chimed another member who announced that her father was a director of British Airways and he would be donating two return tickets to New York flying on Concorde! I turned to look at the person who had, less than a minute earlier, clearly thought she had announced an unbeatable top prize only to see the smile disappear from her face at the realisation that she had just been well and truly 'out-prized'.

The meeting finally came to our part of the agenda. Any prejudice I may have imagined to exist among those present at the prospect of the 'Surrey branch' infiltrating their radio system was quickly dispelled by how enthusiastically they took to the idea. Most of the members seemed to enjoy a fairly privileged way of life, whether at work or doing their 'bit' for The Royal Marsden Hospital and an opportunity to do something more 'hands-on' than the usual fundraising seemed to appeal to them. Their enthusiasm was to prove vital in fulfilling our idea to broadcast to both hospitals. I explained how we thought the link-up could work by having two or three people in the Fulham Road team on each weekday evening. They would not only collect record requests from patients on the wards but we also wanted them to take part in the programmes. This was possible, as the expensive music-quality landline would operate two-way, so it made sense to use that facility by having their teams also broadcasting. Everyone present was overwhelmingly in favour of the link-up and the Junior League immediately offered to cover the cost of the line. Their committee were keen to make it happen without delay and in a very short time they had organised their own programme teams comprising at least three people for each weekday evening's broadcast. In only a couple of months, the landline was installed and linked up to the radio receivers in both hospitals and we were ready to broadcast our first programme to Fulham Road. Their volunteers had found an unused room in the hospital and quickly installed a basic sound mixer complete with microphones and headsets, enabling them to monitor and take part in the programmes.

The launch of Radio Marsden to the patients in Fulham Road was a great success and the few minor technical problems that did arise were quickly solved by our most experienced 'techie' who had gone there with a couple of our other volunteers to oversee that first evening's broadcast. The Fulham Road team visited the wards collecting their own record requests which they then read out on air, as well as arranging their version of our weekly Staff Award. While similar to the Sutton feature, there was one big difference. Their prize to the winner was a very good-quality bottle of wine, compared with Sutton's cheap Pomagne; but after all, they were in Chelsea!

The programme link between the two hospitals lasted beyond my time at Radio Marsden and, in 1992, another voluntary radio service closed due to relocation of their hospital and donated their studio equipment and record library to The Royal Marsden Fulham Road. Once it was all installed, this enabled Fulham Road to provide a higher level of programme input to the benefit of the patients in both hospitals. The 'new and improved' link-up was relaunched by radio broadcasting legend Tony Blackburn and operated successfully for many years until a serious fire engulfed major parts of The Royal Marsden in Fulham Road in January 2008. Such was the devastation, the radio studio along with all its broadcasting equipment was damaged beyond repair by water from the hoses.

Following the fire, the necessary rebuilding of a major part of the hospital took many years and sadly, a Radio Marsden studio was not included in the plans, leaving the Fulham Road patients without a link to hear Radio Marsden.

(From left) Anne Kingswell, me and Maureen Georges host the first programme to be heard by both Sutton and Fulham Road hospitals.

CHAPTER 13

21 years – time to celebrate!

In 1990, Radio Marsden was approaching its 21st birthday and I decided we needed a special programme to celebrate this milestone. Having started in 1969 with that first record request programme presented in front of the patients in a ward lounge, it seemed fitting to reflect on that by putting together a celebrity version. Aiming high, I named it *The Ultimate Royal Request Show* and set about writing individual letters to members of the royal family. I included a brief history of Radio Marsden and what it did currently to entertain the patients. The letters concluded by asking if they would contribute to our 21st birthday programme by naming their favourite piece of music. I avoided requesting an interview or inviting them down to our studio in Sutton, as both were sure to be declined. My objective was to ask them to name a piece of music we could include in our show, as I reckoned we had a better chance of receiving a positive response. Much to my surprise, almost all of the members of the royal family I contacted replied, or rather their private secretaries did on their behalf. That was fair enough as I would have been shocked to receive one saying 'Dear David, It's 'Apache' by The Shadows. Best wishes, Charles'. I really enjoyed reading the replies as they came in and I was surprised that a few of them actually declined to name a piece of music. Whether not wishing to do so was due to royal protocol or it just being too much trouble, I will never know.

One of the first replies I received was from Robert Fellowes, Private Secretary to HM Queen Elizabeth, advising that 'Her Majesty likes many different and varied pieces of music, and I am therefore unable to give you any one specific piece which she would call her favourite'. He even went on to say, 'I am sorry to send you a disappointing reply but hope Radio Marsden's 21st birthday celebrations will be much enjoyed by the patients and staff of both hospitals.' Such was the tone of his letter, I could only guess the scenario when he put my request to Her Majesty, only to be told there were too many to choose from. Did he think, 'Oh come on Ma'am, just pick one.' After more thought, I decided her decision not to name a tune was probably down to royal protocol requiring the sovereign not to favour one over another.

Prince Philip's reply was similar to the Queen's. His secretary said he did not have any particular favourite piece of music that he could give me to announce and he hoped I would understand if he did not contribute to the programme. Rather negative I thought, surely it would have been a lot simpler just to take a stab at one he liked but no, royal protocol again? Possibly, or more likely a matter of sheer cussedness, a trait the prince was well known for.

I was beginning to think we would not have much of a Royal Request Show if the rest of the family sent similar replies to those of The Queen and Prince Philip. Happily, that was not the case when the next letter arrived. It was from the Private Secretary to HM Queen Elizabeth the Queen Mother and contained a totally different reply compared with the first two. He wrote 'at the bidding of Her Majesty', which really impressed me, and went on to say how the Queen Mother was 'pleased to cooperate and had chosen not one, but two of her favourite pieces of music'. These were 'The Londonderry Air' and 'Blaydon Races'. That was more like it, no stuffy protocol from Clarence House, straight to the point and our 21st birthday show had its first music request. That positive letter was soon followed by the reply on behalf of the Prince of Wales. His equerry reported his choice being Chopin's Piano Concerto No.1. The Princess of Wales, Lady Diana, also chose a piece of classical music, Her assistant private secretary and lady-in-waiting describing it in detail as 'Ave Verum' from Faure Requiem, Op.65 No.1. A haunting piece of music, maybe a hint of the tragedy that was to come just seven years later when 'the People's Princess' lost her life in a Paris car crash.

My elation on receiving the choices from the Prince and Princess of Wales was quickly followed by negative replies from Princess Anne and her brother Prince Edward. The secretary to Anne, the Princess Royal, wrote somewhat curtly, 'Her Royal Highness regrets she is unable to assist you in your request, however, I have been asked to convey the Princess's best wishes on the occasion of your 21st anniversary', which was at least something I suppose. Similarly, but in a much longer letter, Prince Edward's assistant explained that, sadly it would not be possible to choose some music and how, 'I am sure you will understand that Prince Edward receives a very large number of similar requests and while it would be unfair to single out one rather than another, it would be impossible to accede to them all.' I thought that somewhat strange of Prince Edward. Five lines to explain how it could not be done but it would have taken just one line to name a piece of music. There was by now only one non-reply. That was to the letter addressed to HRH Prince Andrew. Could this have been just an oversight or an early indication of how his manner would eventually lead to serious embarrassment to other members of the royal family.

In addition to the royals, I also wrote to a few other famous people. These included George Carey, then Archbishop of Canterbury. I was impressed by the reply on his behalf from his 'Secretary for Broadcasting, Press and Communication' which I thought was a great title. He was delighted to forward his choice of music, saying how the Archbishop had deliberately chosen something he hoped would cheer people up. This uplifting song was Judy Garland singing 'Over the Rainbow'. That's the way to do it Archbishop Carey, thank you for that! A positive response also arrived from the prime minister's Press Office advising that Mrs Thatcher had expressed a liking for the song 'Memories' from the musical *Cats* and passing on her congratulations on our 21st birthday. The leader of the opposition, Neil Kinnock provided a long list of his favourite music, from Beethoven and Brahms through to rock and roll and modern jazz, as well as a great deal of operatic and oratorical choral music, mainly Verdi, Handel and Elgar. I began to think he would need an hour's programme all to himself but was reassured by the final paragraph of his letter, where he finally decided on the tenor aria 'Di quella pira' from Verdi's *Il Trovatore*, a truly outstanding piece of music.

Mrs Thatcher's choice of 'Memories' made me think of contacting Andrew Lloyd Webber who wrote the music for *Cats* to see if he had a favourite piece. His response was surprising as he chose 'Some Enchanted Evening' from the musical *South Pacific*. More commercially minded, Richard Branson, not a sir back then but already running his successful airline as well as rapidly expanding his other business interests, chose Phil Collins's 'In the Air Tonight'. By coincidence, a hit released on the Branson-owned Virgin record label, but I kind of respect him for that, always having an eye for business!

With all the request contributions in from the royal family, leading politicians and others, I put together a 50-line running order which was far more ambitious than any of our normal programmes. The chosen music tracks were interspersed with highlights from our first 21 years. These included contributions from other programmes, including recordings from some of our Christmas shows. extracts from interviews with celebrities such as John Cleese and highlights from hospital events Radio Marsden had covered since it started. It also seemed fitting to play Frank Sinatra's 'My Way', our most requested record. The two-and-a-half-hour programme was deemed a success and a fitting way to celebrate the start of our 21st year.

BUCKINGHAM PALACE

15th February, 1990.

Dear Mr. Peschier,

The Queen has commanded me to thank you for your letter of 8th February.

Her Majesty likes many different and varied pieces of music, and I am therefore unable to give you any one specific piece which she would call her favourite.

I am sorry to send you a disappointing reply, but hope Radio Marsden's 21st birthday celebrations will be much enjoyed by the patients and staff of both hospitals.

Yours sincerely,

(ROBERT FELLOWES)

D. Peschier, Esq.

Slightly disappointing reply from Her Majesty The Queen but understandable in her position, being unable to favour one piece over another.

From: Brigadier Clive Robertson

BUCKINGHAM PALACE

23rd February, 1990

Dear Mr Peschier

Thank you for your letter of 8th February 1990.

I am afraid His Royal Highness does not really have any particular favourite piece of music that he can give you to announce. So that I hope you will understand if he does not contribute to your programme on this occasion.

Prince Philip sends his best wishes to Radio Marsden on its 21st Birthday.

Yours sincerely

Clive Robertson

David Peschier, Esq.,

HRH Prince Philip did not appear to be a lover of music.

CLARENCE HOUSE
S.W.1

13th February 1990

Dear Mr Peschier.

I write at the bidding of Queen Elizabeth The Queen Mother to thank you for your letter of 8th February in which you have outlined the imaginative way that Radio Marsden is planning to mark its 21st birthday.

The Queen Mother is pleased to co-operate in the manner you have requested, and would like to suggest "The Londonderry Air" and "Blaydon Races" as the pieces of music of her choice.

Yours sincerely,

Martin Gilliat.

Private Secretary to
Queen Elizabeth The Queen Mother

Excellent selection by the Queen Mother.
Guaranteed to give our patients a smile.

ST. JAMES'S PALACE
LONDON SW1A 1BS

From: The Equerry to H.R.H. The Prince of Wales

28th February 1990

Dear Mr Peschier

Thank you for your letter of 8th February which The Prince of Wales has seen. He has asked me to let you know that his choice to mark Radio Marsden's 21st birthday in Chopin's Piano Concerto No.1.

Yours sincerely

Alistair Watson

Commander Alistair Watson, RN.

David Peschier, Esq.

A well-known piece of classical music chosen by HRH The Prince of Wales.

ST. JAMES'S PALACE
LONDON SW1A 1BS

From: The Assistant Private Secretary and Lady-in-Waiting to H.R.H. The Princess of Wales

21st February 1990

Dear Mr Peschier,

The Princess of Wales has asked me to thank you very much for your letter of 8th February. Her Royal Highness was grateful to you for writing as you did and to hear of the programme you are planning to celebrate the 21st birthday of the Royal Marsden Hospital.

Her Royal Highness has instructed me to say that her favourite piece of music is the "Ave Verum" from Fauré Requiem, op. 65 no. 1.

Yours sincerely

Anne Beckwith-Smith

Miss A. Beckwith-Smith

D. Peschier, Esq.

An unexpectedly very serious piece of music was the choice from HRH Princess of Wales.

BUCKINGHAM PALACE 15 February 1990

Dear Mr. Peschier,

The Princess Royal has asked me to write and thank you for your letter of 8th February.

Her Royal Highness regrets she is unable to assist you in your request, however I have been asked to convey The Princess's best wishes on the occasion of your 21st Anniversary.

Yours sincerely

Madeleine Louloudis

The Hon Mrs Louloudis
Assistant Private Secretary to
HRH The Princess Royal

David Peschier, Esq

Birthday wishes from HRH Princess Anne but sadly, declining to name any music!

From: Lieutenant Colonel Sean O'Dwyer

BUCKINGHAM PALACE

12th February, 1990

Dear Mr Peschier,

The Prince Edward has asked me to thank you for your letter of 8th February in which you invite His Royal Highness to name his favourite piece of music for your programme to mark Radio Marsden's 21st birthday.

I very much regret that sadly it is not possible for His Royal Highness to do as you ask. I am sure you will understand that Prince Edward receives a very large number of similar requests and while it would be unfair to single out one rather than another, it would be impossible to accede to them all.

His Royal Highness is sorry to disappoint you in this way, but sends his best wishes to you and everyone involved with Radio Marsden.

Yours sincerely,

David Peschier Esq.

Following in his sister's footsteps by refusing to name his favourite piece of music, HRH Prince Edward's secretary at least took pains to explain why!

Lambeth Palace London SE1 7JU

David Peschier Esq
Radio Marsden
The Royal Marsden Hospital
Downs Road
SUTTON
Surrey SM2 5PT

19 February 1990

Dear Mr Peschier

The Archbishop is delighted to respond to your request to nominate some favourite music for the 21st birthday of Radio Marsden. He has deliberately chosen something which he hopes will cheer people up - that is, Judy Garland singing "Somewhere over the Rainbow".

Yours sincerely

Eve Keatley
The Archbishop of Canterbury's
Secretary for Broadcasting,
Press and Communications

The Archbishop's uplifting choice of a song from the film The Wizard of Oz.

10 DOWNING STREET

LONDON SW1A 2AA

12 February 1990

Dear Mr Peschier,

I have been asked to reply to your letter of 8 February in which you asked the Prime Minister about her favourite piece of music. I am sorry this is not a personal reply from Mrs Thatcher: I am sure you will appreciate that she receives many letters each day and cannot reply personally to every one.

The Prime Minister has expressed a liking for the song "Memories" from the musical Cats. It would be fine for you to play this as Mrs Thatcher's choice on your programme.

Finally, the Prime Minister is aware of how much pleasure is brought to patients by hospital radio and would, I know, wish me to pass on her congratulations on Radio Marsden's 21st birthday.

Yours sincerely

Kate Waldock

Kate Waldock (Miss)
Press Office

David Peschier Esq
Radio Marsden

Full marks to the prime minister's Press Office for such a perfectly worded reply.

HOUSE OF COMMONS
LONDON SW1A 0AA

The Office of the
Leader of The Opposition

10 April 1990

Dear David Peschier

I am writing to acknowledge your letter to Mr Kinnock and apologise for the delay in replying and to thank you for including him in your special radio programme to mark Radio Marsden's 21st Birthday.

Mr Kinnock is very fond of music and does not have one favourite record but enjoys a great mixture, ranging from Beethoven and Brahms through to 'Rock and Roll' and Modern Jazz with a great deal of operatic and oratoric choral music (mainly Verdi, Handel and Elgar) thrown in, but has chosen the tenor aria "Di quella pira" from Verdi's "Il Travatore".

Mr Kinnock sends his best wishes and congratulations to Radio Marsden.

~~Kind regards~~

Yours sincerely,

R Lane

Leader of the opposition Neil Kinnock submitted a detailed list of all his favourite music before finally settling on a piece by Verdi.

Going through all the replies to compile our 21st birthday programme, the Ultimate Royal Request Show.

And finally...

With ever-increasing work commitments and a growing family, I entered 1991 knowing the time had come to make a decision about my future involvement in Radio Marsden. Twenty-two years had flown by since I first contacted the hospital, asking if they had a voluntary radio service I could join. I certainly never expected my letter would lead me to starting one myself, especially in such a prestigious hospital as The Royal Marsden, but that's what had happened, and each year had brought me fresh challenges as well as many new friends.

The decision I needed to make was simple: stay or go. I took a couple of months to weigh-up the pros and cons of both. Radio Marsden was running really well with a great group of volunteers and our programmes continued to be well received by the patients at both our Sutton and Fulham Road hospitals. With so many people involved, it was beginning to resemble the size of a small business and I had to cope with a constant flow of calls during work hours and at home in the evenings. Sometimes I wished Radio Marsden was still as it was in its early years when we had just a small number of volunteers and a technical side that was simple and easy to understand. It also concerned me to see changes within the hospital. While our League of Friends continued to give us great support, especially by their financial donations, the hospital's management had undergone many changes in my time. Their cooperation and speed of decision-making, while still valuable, was not quite as good as it used to be. It was understandable that the days of sharing a late-night whisky with the administrator may have been over, but I still had a very good relationship with the present incumbent. It was more a case of being on the end of some pressure from a new and enthusiastic nursing manager that gave me concerns. I had the impression, while maybe not wanting to put Radio Marsden under his authority, he was definitely looking for a greater say in what we did. This included him suggesting we start a weekly programme dedicated to ballet music. While rebuffing that idea on the basis of it only being of interest to a small minority of patients, I saw his attempt to influence our programming as a sign of what the future might hold.

Having spent a few weeks deliberating, my options were clear – to either call it a day altogether or relinquish my leadership and remain as an ordinary member working on a weekly programme. When it came to making my final choice, it was down to two factors. Firstly, everything was going well at Radio Marsden, which is always a great time to leave any organisation. Secondly, I had identified a fellow volunteer who I considered had the ability, commitment and, probably most important of all, enthusiasm, to take over from me. I made the decision to leave in May 1991 and was proved right. Barry Alston made a great job of taking my place. Barry did so well, serving as chairperson for many years and as a reliable programme contributor, that he was still there 28 years later! In 2019, Radio Marsden marked its 50th birthday, and I was invited to attend a party to celebrate this milestone. In addition, Barry asked me to join him on his morning show to commemorate the event with a nostalgic look back over our combined half-century of broadcasting.

My visit to the studio took me into that same ground-floor room we had 'hijacked' in 1969 and the memories soon came flooding back. It was also an opportunity for Radio Marsden to demonstrate all the technical advances it had made since I had left. The mixing desk was now linked to a computer. While some programmes, such as those with music requests, were still broadcast live from the studio, presenters could also put together a programme in their home and download it onto the studio's computer for it to be played out at its scheduled time. Thanks to such technology, the station was now able to broadcast programmes 24 hours a day, seven days a week. A vast majority of all types of music are now stored on the computer, but record decks are still needed from time to time to play a track from our library of LPs, which are still there on the shelves, just as they were in my time. One of the biggest changes, similar to most hospital radio services, is that Radio Marsden is now on the internet, broadcasting its programmes to listeners throughout the modern world. All the volunteers I met during my return to the studio, and the many more at the birthday party to commemorate its half-century of broadcasting, still had that same enthusiasm Graham, Andrew and I had during Radio Marsden's early years. I was overwhelmed by the respect they gave me, as its founder, and left the evening's celebrations confident that Radio Marsden was still going strong and in excellent shape to continue broadcasting long into the future.

THE ROYAL MARSDEN HOSPITAL
LONDON & SURREY

DOWNS ROAD
SUTTON SURREY SM2 5PT
TELEPHONE: 081 - 642 6011
EXT 3395

PATRON: HER MAJESTY THE QUEEN

CHAIRMAN:
MARMADUKE J. HUSSEY

GENERAL MANAGER:
PHYLLIS M. CUNNINGHAM

SB/YMP

29th May 1991

Mr D Peschier
Ashwood
37 Hermitage Road
Kenley
Surrey
CR2 5EA

Dear David

Than you for your very kind letter of 19th May 1991, in which you informed me of your retirement from Radio Marsden.

I am or course extremely sad to learn of your retirement from Radio Marsden, but both on a personal level and on behalf of the Hospital I would like to thank you most sincerely for the immense pleasure that your contribution to Radio Marsden has given to the Hospital patients over the last 22 years.

The success of Radio Marsden has been achieved very much as a result of your personal dedication and energies.

Once again on behalf of the Hospital many thanks and best wishes for the future.

Yours sincerely

Stephen Bagot
Operational Services Hospital

Always good to receive appreciation. I was so lucky to deal with excellent hospital managers. From day one through to my retirement, each one gave me their full help and cooperation.

Radio Marsden's volunteers at Sutton 1969–1991

Barry Alston
Fiona Aptel
Martin Ashton
Jenny Bale
Graham Banks
Mandy Barclay
Clare Bedborough
John Bodmin
Roger Bonner
Phil Boys
John Bridger
Michelle Burke
Steve Catton
Emma Chilvers
Matthew Clancy
Chris Cooper
Tammy Cooper
Gill Cox
Terry Day
Shirley Dixon
Alan Donnachie
Vicky Duffy
Tom Ellinor
Iain Ellis
Paul Fillary
Charlotte Fisher
John Fredrickson
Liz Gallacher
Robert Gallacher
Maureen Georges
Andy Hame
Alan Hart
Sarah Hart
Stephen Haylett
Jan Hinson
Paul Holman
Tim Houghton
Richard Hull
Sue Hutton
William Jackson
Jane Keane
Gary Keene
Trish Kinane
Anne Kingswell
Peter Lethbridge
Phil Levy
Joanna Leybourne
Pam Limond
Sue Lockhart
Chris Lovelock
Nick Lucy
Brenda Marsh
Phil Martin
Lee McDonnell

Nikki Mekie
Neal Mullery
Chris Murphy
Keith Newman
James Occomore
Andrew Perkins
David Peschier
Bridgett Phelps
Bob Pix
Ian Porter
Derek Power
Paul Preston
James Pringle
Paul Rand
Fiona Redman
Kevin Rice
Tim Richardson
Andrew Robertson
Gordon Roxburgh
Steven Russell
Brian Sadler
Jane Sanderson
Marge Scivier
Joyce Scriven
Caroline Shaw
Andy Simpson
Mary Simpson
Andrew Smith
Arthur Smith
Graham Smith
Diana Spiller
Peter Stone
Peter Stratford
John Sugden
Pat Sullivan
Caroline Sweeney
Ann Taverner
Tony Taylor
Eirene Theodoris
Keith Warner
Laurie Whatley
Sarah Wilmshurst
Bill Wilson
Keith Woods

Honorary members

Those members of the Sutton branch of The Royal Marsden Hospital's League of Friends who visited the wards each week collecting record requests on behalf of Radio Marsden.

Radio Marsden's volunteers at Fulham Road 1969–1991

Simon Antcliff
Joanna Bird
Belinda Bryant
Sacha Denison-Pender
Pam Edwards
Rebecca Hart
Robert Hayes
Suzi Higman
Neal Hockaway-Ward
Bumble Maclaren
Carmel Moran
James Mullally
Amanda Paul
Jonathan Rawlinson
Sarah Roberts-West
Anna Rogers
Catherine Ronay
Kathy Russell
Julia Sarra
Andrea Thornton
Suzanne Walls
Sarah Wickens

Honorary members

Those members of the Fulham Road Junior and Senior League of Friends who visited the wards each week collecting record requests on behalf of Radio Marsden.

Printed in Great Britain
by Amazon

64885828R00108